Learning and Teaching English

Learning and Teaching English

A COURSE FOR TEACHERS

Cora Lindsay with Paul Knight

OXFORD

UNIVERSITY PRESS

Great Clarendon Street, Oxford OX2 6DP

Oxford University Press is a department of the University of Oxford.
It furthers the University's objective of excellence in research, scholarship,
and education by publishing worldwide in

Oxford New York

Auckland Cape Town Dar es Salaam Hong Kong Karachi
Kuala Lumpur Madrid Melbourne Mexico City Nairobi
New Delhi Shanghai Taipei Toronto

With offices in

Argentina Austria Brazil Chile Czech Republic France Greece
Guatemala Hungary Italy Japan Poland Portugal Singapore
South Korea Switzerland Thailand Turkey Ukraine Vietnam

OXFORD and OXFORD ENGLISH are registered trade marks of
Oxford University Press in the UK and in certain other countries

ISBN: 978 0 19 442275 8 (Book)
ISBN: 978 0 19 442277 2 (Pack)

Printed in China

CONTENTS

ACKNOWLEDGEMENTS

The authors would like to thank the following people for their contributions:

External consultant: Mary Spratt
Senior consultant: Professor Christopher Candlin
Project manager: Ian Spratley

Contributors to the text: Rena Basak, Ann Hewings, Felicity O'Dell, Liz Oldham, Carolyn McKinney, Anne Timson

Recording actors: Clive Hayward, Rebecca Deren, Sophie Hein, Eddie Matthews

Case study teachers: Alastair Douglas, Katherine Hill, Hana Švecová, Jan Madakbas, Yuko Kikuchi, Małgorzata Kułakowska, Melissa Lamb, Marta Perez-Yarza, Silvana Rampone, Catherine Xiang

Illustrations: Ann Harvey

Particular thanks go to Bruce Wade, our editor at OUP, whose suggestions and work on this project have been infinitely useful.

INTRODUCTION

Learning and Teaching English is for people who wish to develop their expertise in English language teaching. It is for teachers at all stages of their career – trainee teachers, newly qualified teachers, and teachers with some experience. It is for teachers of children, young adults, and adults.

The book is a self-study guide which readers can work through at their own pace. There are optional activities which encourage the reader to think about topics for themselves. The answers are in the back. The book can also provide the basis for a face-to-face course, and many of the activities provide a good springboard for group discussion.

The book gives an overall view of learning, the English language, and ELT practices and is useful for readers who are preparing for a teaching qualification – the Cambridge ESOL Teaching Knowledge Test (TKT), the CELTA qualification, and other equivalent examinations.

Contents

The book covers the principal aspects of ELT. The first chapter on teaching and learning languages considers the ways we learn a language, looks at what makes a good language learner, and describes the ways in which teaching and learning relate to each other. In the chapter on methodology we look at the methods and ideas that have shaped teaching practices and the relevance and usefulness they have today. There is a chapter on language which looks at the English language from the smallest components – individual sounds and letters – and how they build up to form syllables, words, phrases, sentences, and finally the extraordinary range of written and spoken forms that English takes. The chapter then goes on to look at how we can help learners understand the language system and develop their ability to use it to communicate successfully inside and outside the classroom. The book then looks in detail at each of the four skills – listening, speaking, reading, and writing – and considers first how these skills are used in the 'real' world and then applies this understanding to what we do in the classroom. There is a section on planning, for individual lessons, a sequence of lessons, and finally a complete course or syllabus. The section describes all the important elements that make up a lesson plan and shows how to put these into a logical and effective sequence of activities. Finally, there is a section on ways of assessing and evaluating learners – what we should assess and effective and motivating ways of understanding what learners can and cannot do.

Activities

Each chapter includes a number of activities. These activities are entirely optional but are an opportunity for the reader to consider the ideas in each chapter in more detail. They include activities that help the reader to develop a deeper understanding of the language system, give them greater insights into what they do in the classroom, and help them to understand the learner and how to encourage and foster more effective learning. Where there is a possible correct answer, it can be found in the answer key at the back of the book.

Portfolio work

There are a number of optional tasks throughout the book entitled 'Portfolio work'. These are longer activities which ask readers to try out a teaching idea for real in the classroom and keep a record or portfolio of the results. Readers can also use the portfolio to record:

– responses to the activities in the book
– samples of activities that they themselves have tried out with their classes
– evaluations – how well (or not) certain activities worked with their classes and how they might be improved
– their own feelings about teaching
– lesson plans and details of activity sequences
– any extra reading material or websites they might have found helpful.

As well as providing readers with a valuable record of their own work, and the responses of their students, a portfolio can in some cases serve as final assessment, or part of a final assessment, in any qualification linked to the content of the book.

Case studies

After the chapter on assessment, there are nine case studies based on authentic interviews with teachers from around the world who talk about their experiences of and opinions about language and language learning, teaching methods and teaching, planning, and assessment. Each case study is on the CD and is followed in the book by questions which help the reader to check whether they have understood the main points and encourage them to relate their own experiences or opinions to those of the teachers. The questions are set out in a format similar to TKT activities and include multiple choice, sequencing, matching, and true/false questions.

Glossary

At the end of the book we list the key ELT terms that have been used in each chapter. This is aimed to help readers master the jargon of language teaching so that they can read and discuss issues related to their work and help them if they are planning to take the TKT or other teaching qualifications. Each term is cross-referenced with the page it occurs on in the main section of the book.

Classroom language

The book includes a section which gives examples of some of the most common types of classroom language. This includes different types of interaction – teacher to learner, learner to teacher, and learner to learner, and key teacher language for classroom management, asking questions and eliciting, providing encouragement and correction, and developing a rapport with their class. This section can also be heard on the CD.

Further reading list

There is a list of recommended books which go into more detail about the nine topics covered in the book.

We hope you will enjoy this book and find it useful in your teaching career.

1 LEARNING AND TEACHING ENGLISH

In this chapter we explore:

– the relationship between learning and teaching
– factors which affect language learning
– the language learning process
– language learning **aims**.

Learning

Learning can take place both inside and outside the classroom. It can be an informal process – picking up words from the TV, magazines, books, or friends; or it can be a formal process – attending lessons and taking part in classroom activities where language and skills are introduced and practised.

The learner may be conscious that they are learning something, for example, they use a bilingual dictionary to check the **meaning** of a word or ask a friend to explain. Learning may also happen without the learner being aware of it. They copy expressions and phrases from other people without consciously checking the meaning or analyzing how the language is used.

ACTIVITY 1

Think about your experience of learning English. How did you learn? What effect did your English teachers and the way they taught have on you? Have your experiences as a language learner affected your teaching? If so, in what way?

Active learners

Learners can be active or passive. **Active learners** develop positive habits that allow them to learn more quickly and efficiently. For example, they:

- give themselves as much opportunity as possible to encounter new language
- actively notice and analyze new language and incorporate it into the language they use
- use the new language as much as possible inside and outside the classroom
- take every opportunity to practise the **four skills**
- use study techniques, such as making **vocabulary** lists, to help their learning
- are prepared to experiment, make guesses, and take risks, even if this involves making mistakes
- have confidence in themselves and their ability to learn
- are aware of their own weak areas and gaps in their learning
- monitor their own language use and self-correct where necessary.

When learners encounter a new word in English there are several ways to find out what it means. They can:

- try to relate it to words in their L1, for example, 'rectangle' is similar to 'retângulo' in Portuguese, 'rectángulo' in Spanish, 'rektangel' in Swedish
- break down the parts of the word, i.e. 'rect' and 'angle'
- use visual clues if there are any, for example, a rectangular-shaped object
- look the word up in a bilingual dictionary
- ask someone to explain the meaning
- guess the word from the **context**, for example, someone is talking about cardboard boxes
- guess the word from the **text** – see the activity below.

In each of these examples learners are actively doing something to relate the new word (and new knowledge) to their existing knowledge.

ACTIVITY 2

Look at the text below and try to decide what the invented words in *italics* mean. What clues are there to help you work out the meaning?

Since it was hot John took off his thick *blaggar* as soon as he came into the house. He switched on the kettle to make himself a cup of hot *cofty*. He put on his *homeyshoes* and took his cofty into the living room where he settled down in his *bestingest* armchair. He breathed a *fuff* of relief. It had been a long and *dirky* day.

You can use activities like this with your learners. Lewis Carroll's poem *Jabberwocky*, which has many invented words, is a great text to use for this.

As regards learning in the classroom, learners also need to develop good habits such as:

– taking an active part in activities by asking questions and initiating exchanges with other learners and the teacher
– making notes and keeping records of what has been learnt
– reviewing and consolidating
– completing homework
– coming to class on time and prepared.

The classroom is also where the combination of learning and teaching takes place.

PORTFOLIO WORK

Choose the strongest learner in one of your classes and consider if they fit the profile of a good language learner described above. Look at one of the weaker learners in your class. What do you think you can do to help them improve their language learning skills?

Teaching

The teacher's job is to help learners learn. This relates both to the formal classroom process and learning outside the classroom.

Teachers are responsible for a large amount of what happens in the classroom – what is taught, the resources used, the type and order of activities, classroom management, assessment, feedback, correction, and so on. It is also part of the teacher's job to encourage learners to take responsibility for their own learning and become 'active learners'. An effective teacher:

– understands learners' language needs and responds to them positively
– designs lessons which reflect the learners' needs and develop their communicative skills
– monitors and corrects sensitively
– provides feedback and encouragement when appropriate

– tells learners not to worry about making mistakes – this is part of the learning process
– encourages good learning habits inside and outside the classroom
– keeps track of progress, gaps in learners' ability, and repeated errors
– creates an 'input-rich environment' in the classroom, for example, by putting lots of pictures with English text on the walls
– encourages learners to read English texts or listen to the radio in English, for example the BBC World Service Online, CDs, and audio cassettes. Television programmes, both terrestrial and digital, can also be an excellent source of input.

The relationship between learning and teaching is complicated and often not direct. Learners often don't learn what we teach and equally often learn what we don't teach. One way to help overcome this problem is to create a positive relationship between yourself and your learners.

Scaffolding

One of the ways in which teachers can help learners is by providing carefully structured support. This support is sometimes described as **scaffolding**: the teacher supports the efforts of the learner, guiding them in the right direction, until the knowledge and understanding they have built is strong enough for the 'scaffolding' to be taken away. Scaffolded learning will involve the teacher in:

– designing activities which break down the learning task into manageable stages
– designing activities that build on previous activities
– helping learners see how the knowledge they already have is useful for making sense of the new knowledge
– deciding when learners are ready to move on to the next stage.

An understanding of the active nature of learning and of the principles of scaffolding can influence our general approach to teaching in a number of ways. Whatever activities your learners are involved in you should encourage them to think about what they are doing. You must be careful to move in stages from what your learners know, towards the new knowledge you are trying to help them learn.

Active and scaffolded learning are shown below in an example from a language classroom. Look at the steps in the lesson. Notice how the teacher has planned activities which scaffold the learning so that learners move from the point of being able to say 'My name is … and I live in …', to being able to exchange information on their names, their addresses, and their telephone numbers. The scaffolding is achieved through input from the teacher, pair work, individual work, and whole-class work.

Step 1

The teacher tells the class the aim of lesson – to learn how to exchange information about themselves in a conversation.

Step 2

The teacher starts by going round the class with each learner saying 'My name is … and I live in …'. This revises the two expressions and helps build confidence.

Step 3

The teacher models the questions 'What is your name?' and 'Where do you live?' The learners repeat them. The teacher gets specific learners to ask and answer the questions. The questions are written on the board. Learners walk around the room asking and answering the questions.

giving

Step 4

The teacher models the question 'What is your telephone number?' Learners repeat it. The question is written on the board. Vocabulary necessary to answer the question (numbers up to 9) is revised and written on board. Learners practise in **open pairs** asking 'What is your telephone number?' and answering with the right number. The learner asking the question writes down the number and the other learner checks if it is correct. Learners repeat the **activity** with different partners.

giving

new   giving it

Step 5

The teacher uses the question 'Where do you live?' to find out how much of the vocabulary for this the learners already know, for example, 'road', 'street', 'avenue', 'square'. The teacher writes up the words they need to use in the learners' L1. Learners work with a partner to look up the English words for these in a bilingual dictionary. The teacher writes the English words from learners' answers on the board.

assessment

giving it

Step 6

The teacher and selected learners model a 'question and answer' dialogue in which names, addresses, and telephone numbers are exchanged. Learners practise with a partner. The questions are left on the board at first but later rubbed off. Learners draw a table in their notebooks with the headings: name, address, and telephone. Learners exchange information with others in the class and write down their names, addresses, and telephone numbers in their notebooks. This can be used for revision and further work in another lesson.

setting

USING it → remove visual support

PORTFOLIO WORK

Look through your coursebook or any lesson plans you have used recently.
Do they scaffold the new language learning points sufficiently? What extra stages might you add?

As we can see, there are at least two ways learning can take place. Learners can take responsibility for their own learning – develop learning strategies, use opportunities to communicate, and self-monitor and correct. At the other end of the spectrum, the teacher takes responsibility – provides input, the opportunity to practise, and gives feedback and correction. Learning takes place in a variety of ways between these two parameters.

Factors which affect language learning

The relationship between teaching and learning is a key factor in whether learning takes place effectively. There are also other factors which mean that some people learn more easily and more quickly than others.

ACTIVITY 3

Consider the following statements about language learning and tick either 'true', 'false', or 'it depends' for each one. Then look at the comments below.

	True	False	It depends
1 Everyone can learn a foreign language.	☐	☐	☐
2 Some people find it easier than others to learn a language.	☐	☐	☐
3 Children learn foreign languages more easily than adults.	☐	☐	☐

4 People learn a language best by being immersed in it. ☐ ☐ ☐

5 Grammar is the most important element of
   learning a language ☐ ☐ ☐

6 You shouldn't start speaking in a foreign language
   until you can say things correctly. ☐ ☐ ☐

Innate ability

Everyone has the potential to learn a first and second language. A significant proportion of the world's population is at least bilingual – many people can speak three languages or more.

Aptitude

Some people do seem to learn more easily than others. However, there is no scientific evidence that there is a biological difference in people's aptitude for learning. It is more likely to be a combination of some or all of the following factors.

Motivation

One of the most important factors is how motivated learners are to learn English. **Motivation** can be analyzed in terms of whether it is **intrinsic** or **extrinsic**. Intrinsic motivation refers to the individual learner's wish to learn or enjoyment in learning; extrinsic motivation to a learner's need to learn because of external factors such as employment, social pressure, academic requirements, and so on. A mismatch between the two, i.e. someone who has to learn but doesn't want to, can create problems and lead to ineffective learning. Motivation can be supported by:

– making a point of looking for texts that appeal to learners' interests
– trying to create a classroom culture that encourages learners to feel confident about taking risks and using the new language
– holding an open discussion with learners about the purposes of learning English, their own motivations, and their views about the task of learning a foreign language
– using questionnaires or other kinds of enquiry to discover which language learning activities your learners find the most enjoyable and productive
– using class questionnaires to find out what your learners' want from a course
– involving learners in decisions about the classroom learning process.

Age

It is widely believed that young children learn a second language more easily than older children or adults. But recent research has shown that teenagers are often the most successful language learners, and that older adults can be very successful too. Children often concentrate and learn best if they are doing a variety of activities that activate all their senses – touch, taste, smell, sight, and sound.

Proximity of L1 to English

The global variety of languages means that some have a lot in common with English while others are different in many important ways. Here are some of the key features:

– alphabet
– sound system
– written form
– script and layout
– grammar
– social and cultural factors

ACTIVITY 4

Make a list of as many languages as you can and rank them in terms of how similar they are to English.

Opportunity to use the target language

One good way of learning is by **immersion** in the environment where the **target language** is used – being able to or having to use it in your daily life. However, many people have learnt to speak and read English very well without ever having been immersed in an English-speaking culture. If learners get lots of practice using English in the classroom, they can make significant progress.

Learning strategies

As we have seen, there are a wide variety of ways the learner can speed up and improve the way they learn.

Learner types

Different learners learn more effectively depending on how they are able to learn, for example:

– visual learners prefer to see words and pictures
– auditory learners like listening and talking with other people
– tactile learners like touching and manipulating objects
– kinaesthetic learners like movement
– field-independent learners like to concentrate on the details and rules

– field-dependent learners are more interested in getting across the general meaning than learning rules
– reflective learners like to focus on **accuracy** and need time to get things right.

Relationship to teaching

As we have seen, the way a teacher teaches is an important factor and this also relates to learner types, for example, some learners may prefer a teacher who gives them lots of rules about the language. Other learners may prefer a teacher who encourages them to communicate freely and experiment using English.

Relationship to the teacher

Personal relationships also play a big part in classroom learning. A good rapport between teacher and learner is likely to be beneficial to the learning process.

Relationship with other learners

How the learner feels about the other learners in the class or group can affect language learning. It is best if learners feel comfortable with each other and are prepared to co-operate in learning. For example, if one learner dominates and doesn't give others a chance to participate, this makes learning more difficult for the less dominant individuals.

Embarrassment and anxiety

Nobody likes to make a fool of themselves in public, and learners often feel that they will do this when trying to speak or read out loud in English. But unless they try to use English to communicate, they will not learn quickly.

Self-confidence

It is often easier for people who are confident in themselves to learn a language than it is for those who have low self-confidence. This is linked to 'fear of embarrassment' because learners who are confident will be more prepared to take risks using the new language than learners with a low level of confidence.

Attitudes towards language learning

In some countries, learning another language is considered a normal and easy thing to do, while in others it is considered an unusual and demanding task. These differences are well illustrated by the Netherlands and Britain. In the Netherlands, most people expect to learn at least two languages, and by the time they are teenagers many Dutch children speak excellent English. In Britain, on the other hand, few young children learn to speak a foreign language, and most teenagers consider language learning a very hard task.

Attitudes towards English and English-speaking countries

The learning process can be affected by learners' attitudes towards English and towards L1 speakers of English and their culture(s); this can affect learners' motivation in particular. Some people associate learning English with learning about the culture and values of English-speaking countries. For some learners who may reject the culture and values this can be demotivating. Nowadays this is less significant as English is used extensively as a world or international language, not associated with any one country.

Status and value of the target language in the country

The status of a language refers to its position in relation to other languages. Is the language highly valued or not? Learners may be more motivated to learn a language which they think has high status and practical value.

Learning theories

'Grammar is the most important element of learning a language' is an example of a learning theory that directly affects learners. Expert opinions on how important grammar teaching is for learning language change regularly. It also depends on learner types. For young children grammar teaching is likely to be less useful than giving them practical experience and helping them develop vocabulary. But for older learners, knowledge of how the language works in terms of sentence building, word endings, and the relationship between words is essential for them to be able to express themselves.

'You shouldn't start speaking in a foreign language until you can say things correctly' is simply wrong: it contradicts the principle of active learning.

Learners should be encouraged to use English to try to communicate as soon as they begin learning it. This can be very motivating. Also, they will learn from their efforts, and from constructive feedback provided by their teacher.

The language learning process

The language learning process can be divided into five stages:

INPUT → NOTICING → RECOGNIZING PATTERNS AND RULE MAKING → USE AND RULE MODIFICATION → AUTOMATING

Learning can be an autonomous process, i.e. the learner learns independently of the formal classroom process, or a collaborative process, where the learner and teacher work together. Both processes are described in the five stages below.

Input

First of all learners need **input**. Input is all the target language that a learner is exposed to, both spoken and written, inside or outside the classroom, formal (from a classroom activity that introduces new language) or informal (from other classroom activities or from something heard or read outside the classroom). Sources of input can be the teacher, friends, newspapers, TV programmes, the Internet, films, coursebooks, novels, dictionaries, and so on. Some input will contain language which the learner doesn't understand and/or cannot use.

Noticing

Learners will **notice** only some of the language they are exposed to. Some of this they will already know and some may be new. In this case the learner may notice a gap in their learning, or the gap might be brought to their attention by their teacher. For example, an elementary learner might start to notice that some verbs end in '-ed'. Alternatively the teacher might decide that their learners are at the stage where they are ready to put together expressions using the past tense and introduce the '-ed' ending using a written and /or spoken text.

Recognizing patterns and rule making

The learners might then start to notice that the **pattern** of these verbs often refers to the past and start to develop a rule for themselves – 'verbs ending in '-ed' refer to things that happen in the past.'

In the classroom, the teacher might tell the learners the rule and then give them a chance to use it in a writing or speaking activity, for example, telling a short story. Alternatively the teacher might give learners examples of '-ed' being used in a conversation or story and encourage them to discover patterns and rules for themselves.

Use and rule modification

The individual learner, having generated their own rule, starts to use the rule to produce their own sentences. As their rule does not include the exceptions of irregular verbs, they will make mistakes. They might then be corrected and modify the rule to include irregularities. Alternatively they might notice for themselves that some verbs referring to the past do not end in '-ed' and modify their rule accordingly.

In the classroom the teacher has the choice of giving their learners the whole set of rules for forming verbs in the past tense or limiting the explanation to regular forms first and providing a further explanation when irregular forms start to occur in texts.

Automating

Eventually the learner will be able to refer to the past using both regular and irregular verbs without consciously thinking of which ending is needed. At this point the language has become **automatic** – by which we mean that the learner is beginning to use English intuitively, more like the way they use their L1. This means that language has to be stored in the memory so that it is immediately accessible and remains there. Learners need to keep using new rules and language in order to maintain this stage.

ACTIVITY 5

How does the process described above compare with your own experience of:

– learning English   – teaching English?

Language learning aims

Learners need to balance the following four aspects of their language ability:

FLUENCY   ACCURACY

COMPLEXITY   APPROPRIACY

Fluency

Learners need to be able to choose language and put it together into a comprehensible **message** quickly enough to fit the flow of conversation. In order to maintain **fluency** learners need to adapt what they want to say to their language level and develop strategies to talk around what they cannot express directly.

Accuracy

At the same time, they need to produce a message that is accurate enough in terms of the word order, words endings, pronunciation, and so on for the listener to understand. This does not mean that learners have to be 100% accurate all the time. An approximation of the 'ideal' way to say something often works and learners should be encouraged to take risks and use language at the edge of their language level.

Complexity

As they learn, learners develop the range of expressions they can use so that they can produce language that fits the situations they are in more and more precisely. This range often indicates their actual level, though this must be balanced by the ability to use the language reasonably fluently and accurately. It is the teacher's job to help learners achieve this balance as they progress.

Appropriacy

The learner's choice of language must fit the situation. A learner may be able to produce a very accurate, complex sentence and fit it into to the flow of conversation without hesitation, but it might be entirely inappropriate.

ACTIVITY 6

Think of an example of a learner expressing themselves by talking round a word or structure that they don't know. Think of an example of language that is accurate but inappropriate.

Summary

Effective learning is the result of the partnership between learner and teacher with both taking the responsibilities appropriate to their roles. In order to fulfil their role teachers must have a sound knowledge of the language system and the four skills. We will be looking at details of these in chapters 3 to 8.

Case study

Go to the 'Case study' section at the back of the book and listen to a teacher talk about their experiences of teaching and learning.

2 TEACHING METHODS AND IDEAS

In this chapter we explore some of the main teaching **methods** and ideas that have influenced the way we teach English. These include:

– the Grammar-Translation Method
– the Direct Method
– Audiolingualism
– Communicative Language Teaching
– Task-Based Learning.

ACTIVITY 1

Was the way you learnt English or another language influenced by a particular method? As a teacher do you use a particular method?

We are now going to look at the details of the methods in terms of their history, their main features, and the current influence they have on teaching and learning.

The Grammar-Translation Method

Background

The Grammar-Translation Method was developed in the 18th century and was introduced as a way of teaching modern languages to school children. The method itself came from the way individual learners studied classical languages such as Greek and Latin. This was done mainly by studying the grammar in detail and translating texts from the original into the learner's language.

Features

Sentences and longer texts are translated both to and from the learner's first language. Little or no attention is paid to the ability to speak or communicate. Long lists of words are commonly memorized without being used in a sentence. Grammar rules are given a lot of attention, especially word endings and sentence formation. The teacher does not have to be able to speak the **target language** in order to teach.

Current status

Grammar-translation is still used to some extent in more traditional schools. Here are some problems that can occur:

– Learners learn about the language, rather than how to use the language.
– Learners do not get much, if any, opportunity to develop listening and speaking skills.
– Vocabulary is made more difficult to use because it is usually taught in isolated lists.
– Using correct grammar is given more emphasis than being able to communicate with someone.
– The attention given to grammatical accuracy and translation may be demotivating for some learners.

One advantage the method does have is that teachers develop an awareness of grammar rules, which is not necessarily the case with Communicative Language Teaching (CLT). One feature of the Grammar-Translation Method which is still in general use is the translation of words and phrases from the target language into the learners' first language. This can be an efficient way of learning some types of vocabulary and a help in learning some grammatical **structures.** On the other hand, it is not always possible to translate a word or structure accurately and the act of translating limits the extent to which learners think in English.

PORTFOLIO WORK

Select a grammatical structure which your learners need and choose five sentences in English which show this structure. Ask your learners to translate them into their first language (L1). Compare the pattern in the two languages.

To what extent does this type of activity lead to learning? How does it compare with more contemporary methods of teaching?

The Direct Method

Background

The Direct Method was developed in the early 20th century in order to overcome the problems connected with grammar-translation.

Features

The Direct Method moved away from translation and introduced the idea of lessons being conducted only in the target language. The meaning of words and structures was communicated 'directly' through mime and gestures, and practised in question-and-answer exchanges between the teacher and learners. Learners were not taught grammar rules but worked them out for themselves.

Current status

The Direct Method was an important step forward – the use of the target language as the language of instruction underpins a lot of teaching today. It was developed from the 1920s onwards into a more sophisticated method called Situational Language Teaching. This centred on the oral practice of carefully graded structures. One key feature was that the language was explained using a situation. (See Figure 2.1 for an example.) The language was practised using guided repetition, **dictation**, **drills**, and oral-based reading and writing **tasks**.

READING-TEXT THIRTEEN

§1

The time is half past two. Mrs West is in the kitchen. She is putting her apron on.

There is a gas-cooker in the kitchen. Mrs West is standing near it. She is going to turn the gas on in the oven and light the gas. Then she is going to make a cake.

2.30 p.m.

What has Mrs West done? She has put her apron on. She is wearing the apron now, over her dress. She has lit the gas in the oven. She has put a lot of things on the table: a jug of milk, some butter, some eggs, a bag of flour, a bag of sugar, some raisins and some currants.

She is going to mix all these things together in a bowl. Then she is going to put the mixture into a baking-tin.

2.35 p.m.

The time is now a quarter to three. What has Mrs West just done? She has mixed all the things together now. She has put the mixture into the baking-tin. She is not standing near the table now. She has just opened the oven door. She is going to put the tin into the oven and close the oven door.

2.45 p.m.

*Figure 2.1 A page from an English coursebook published in 1964 (*Oxford Progressive English*).*

Audiolingualism

habits

Background

Audiolingualism was developed in the 1950s and 1960s when it was believed that learning a language was similar to learning new habits. Language was described in terms of the way it was structured – individual sounds and letters, words, structures, and sentence types. Learners were expected to learn the grammar of the new language not by learning rules but by producing the language accurately by responding to stimuli. These stimuli were prompts which would lead the learner to produce particular sentences. Speaking and listening were seen as the basis of language learning with reading and writing coming later.

Features

A common feature of the audiolingual classroom was the drill. A drill was an activity where the teacher provided prompts and the learners would produce a sentence using the appropriate grammatical structure, for example:

TEACHER   [holding up a picture of a post office] Where's Mary going?
LEARNER   She's going to the post office.

Here are some features of a typical lesson:

– Lessons often began with **dialogues**.
– The emphasis was on the **form** (or structure) of language rather than on content and meaning.
– Grammatical structures were taught in a particular order – structures which were thought to be simpler were introduced before more complicated ones.
– Correct pronunciation was strongly encouraged from the beginning.
– Vocabulary was severely limited in the early stages.
– The teacher made a great effort to prevent errors.
– Drills were the main way new language was practised (see Figure 2.2).

Current status

Some language teachers find drills useful for practising sentence patterns. They can be especially valuable in getting elementary learners to build their confidence in speaking. However, nowadays the usefulness of drills is regarded as limited in that they do not give the learners an opportunity to interact naturally with other speakers.

ACTIVITY 2

Have you ever learnt or taught English using the audiolingual method? Was it effective? What, if any, problems did you have?

4   Drill:

T: *I usually have water with my meals.*
T: *sometimes*
T: *I sometimes have water with my meals.*
T: *wine*
T: *I sometimes have wine with my meals.*
T: *I usually have water with my meals*
    Repeat!
C: *I usually have water with my meals.*

Continue:
sometimes
wine
He
always
They
beer
She
never

5   Drill:

T: *He usually has water, . . . tonight/champagne.*
T: *He usually has water, but tonight he's having champagne.*
Continue:
He usually has water, . . . tonight/wine.
He usually has eggs, . . . tonight/steak.
He usually has beer, . . . tonight/whisky.
He usually smokes cigarettes, . . . tonight/cigars.
He usually eats at home, . . . tonight/restaurant.

6   Drill:

T: *Please don't call me Mr/Mrs/Miss (Smith). My friends always call, me (John/Mary).*
Get the students to do the same using their own names.
Prompt by addressing students by their title and surname.
T: *Now, Mr Schmidt. . . .*
S: *Please don't call me Mr Schmidt. My friends always call me Franz.*

7   Drill:

T: *She doesn't like restaurants.*
T: *They*
T: *They don't like restaurants.*
T: *Do they . . . ?*
T: *Do they like restaurants?*
T: *She doesn't like restaurants.*
    Repeat!
C: *She doesn't like restaurants.*

Continue:
They
Do they . . . ?
he
you
pubs
Why . . . ?
he
they

*Figure 2.2 A page from an English coursebook published in 1978 (*Streamline Departures*).*

PORTFOLIO WORK

Choose a structure to practise with your class using a drill – there are more details about using drills in chapter 5 on p.61. Decide on the type of drill to use and try it out with your class.

Make notes on how effective the drill was, whether there were any limitations to using the drill, and how it affected the learners' motivation. Would you use drills in the future?

Communicative Language Teaching

Background

Communicative Language Teaching (CLT) started in the late 1960s and continues to evolve. It is not actually a method but an approach to teaching based on the view that learning a language means learning how to communicate effectively in the world outside the classroom. It developed mainly as a reaction to the limitations of previous methods which put little, if any, emphasis on the ability to communicate or interact. It was also influenced by developments in the way the language was described – taking into account the communicative **function** of language, i.e. that we use language to do things like suggest, invite, agree, request, criticize, predict, and so on.

Features

Here are some of the main features of CLT:

– The goal is to learn to communicate in the target language.
– There is an emphasis on meaning and *using* the language rather than on the structure and form of the language.
– **Oral** and written activities may be used from the start, for example, **role plays**, dialogues, games, and problem-solving.
– One role for the teacher is that of a 'facilitator' who helps learners to communicate in English and motivates them to work with the language.
– Learners often interact with each other through **pair** or **group work**.
– The four skills are developed simultaneously.

Many CLT classrooms use a Presentation–Practice–Production or **PPP** model of teaching. The teacher first 'presents' the new language, possibly by playing a recorded dialogue or getting the learners to read a written text. Then the learners 'practise' the new language in a controlled way, possibly by completing written exercises using the new language or in controlled pair work practising similar dialogues. Finally, the learners 'produce' the language in a freer activity that allows them to communicate, hopefully using the language they have just studied.

An example of a PPP lesson at an elementary level would be introducing the language of giving directions. First, the teacher might present the target language by asking the learners to listen to a recording of someone asking for directions and to complete some sentences on a worksheet. The sentences would include the language of directions. The learners then practise this language using simple maps provided by the teacher (see Figure 2.3).

EVERYDAY ENGLISH
Directions 1

1 Look at the street map. Where can you buy these things?

| some aspirin   a CD   a plane ticket   a newspaper   a book   some stamps |

[street map showing: bank, Chinese restaurant, bookshop, bus stop, park, Queen Lane, swimming pool, supermarket, Park, chemist, public toilet, supermarket, YOU ARE HERE, car park, cinema, Church, music shop, phone box, bank, Street, pub, travel agent, Italian restaurant, newsagent, post office, post box]

2 **T 5.6** Listen to the conversations and complete them.

1 A Excuse me! Is _____ a chemist _____ here?
   B Yes. It's over _____ .
   A Thanks.

2 A _____ me! Is there a _____ near here?
   B Yes. _____ _____ Church Street. Take the first _____ _____
      _____ right. It's _____ _____ the music shop.
   A Oh yes. Thanks.

3 A Excuse me! Is there a _____ near here?
   B There's a Chinese one in Park Lane _____ _____ the bank, and
      there's an Italian one in Church Street next to the _____ _____ .
   A Is that one _____ ?
   B No. Just two minutes, that's all.

4 A Is there a post office near here?
   B Go straight ahead, and it's _____ _____ left, _____ _____ the pub.
   A Thanks a lot.

Practise the conversations with a partner.

3 Make more conversations with your partner. Ask and answer about these places:

• a bookshop
• a cinema
• a bank
• a phone box
• a public toilet
• a music shop
• a supermarket
• a bus stop
• a park
• a swimming pool
• a post box
• a pub

4 Talk about where *you* are. Is there a chemist near here? Is it far? What about a bank/a post office/ a supermarket?

Figure 2.3 A page from an English coursebook published in 2000 (Headway Elementary).

Finally, they can produce the language more freely by giving directions to places they actually know, possibly using real maps brought into the classroom for this purpose by the teacher or drawn by the learners themselves.

Role playing is a common feature of the CLT classroom and involves the learners acting as someone else, for example, a customer, a ticket sales person, etc. in a situation where they need to use English, for example, to order a meal or buy tickets at a railway station. In this case, one learner would be the customer asking questions about the train times and ticket prices, etc, while another would be the ticket seller giving the information.

ACTIVITY 3

Imagine you are preparing your learners for the following role plays. Note down for each of the situations below some of the language you would teach before the role play. Take into account the learners' age and level.

1 Meeting someone for the first time   Young beginners
2 Planning a night out with friends   Teenage intermediate learners

---

The original PPP model has been developed and modified since it was first introduced and no longer represents CLT as the only teaching model. Language can be introduced and practised in a variety of ways. Learners can be encouraged to discover the patterns of the language for themselves through reading or listening to texts and answering questions about the patterns of the language contained in the texts. For example:

Who's going to the cinema?   We are.
Who'll go to the cinema?   We will.
Who's been to the cinema?   We have.
Who goes to the cinema?   We do.
Who went to the cinema?   We did.

How do we give a short response to a 'wh' question? (use the full form of the original auxiliary or 'do' if there is no auxiliary; the main verb and indirect object are omitted.)

An alternative to this would be to give the learners a rule and then give them an exercise to practise the application of the rule. For example:

To make a comparison we add '-er' to words of one syllable, for example, 'tall' → 'taller', and 'more' before words of three syllables, for example, 'beautiful' → 'more beautiful'. For words of one syllable ending in 'y' we change the 'y' to 'i' and add '-er', for example, 'happy' → 'happier'.

1 John is (short) than Paul.
2 Your boots are (dirty) than mine.
3 This garden is (attractive) than the other one.

The Test-Teach-Test (TTT) approach is useful when the teacher is not sure whether the learners are familiar with a particular item of language. For example, the class are asked to work in pairs and arrange a time to meet using a pre-prepared schedule. The learners do the activity and the teacher monitors and notes down the use of tenses referring to the future, for example, 'I will meet John tomorrow', 'I will go shopping on Saturday', etc.

Based on these results the teacher decides which areas the learners need to do more work on and devises an activity that introduces the present continuous to talk about arrangements ('I'm meeting John tomorrow.') and 'going to' to talk about intentions ('I'm going to go shopping on Saturday'). The learners then do a practice activity similar to the original one.

Current status

CLT is very widely used in language teaching all over the world. It has shifted the focus in language teaching from learning *about* the language to learning to communicate *in* the language. However, there are problems associated with CLT:

– The emphasis on pair and group work can create problems in some classes. Some learners, particularly adults, think it is a waste of time talking to other L2 speakers rather than a native-speaker teacher.
– Native-speaker teachers do not need to know much about the language in order to become teachers.
– The approach can lead to too much emphasis on speaking and listening.
– Dividing the language up into discrete units under the headings of 'vocabulary', 'grammar', and 'functions' and the four skills is misleading. Communication involves using all these elements simultaneously.
– Learners do not necessarily learn what they are taught, i.e. the discrete language items, in the order that they are taught.

The most serious criticism of CLT is that it is not as effective as it claims to be. A lot of learners complete their studies but are still unable to communicate in English. One reaction to this has been to change the learning focus from the content, i.e. the structures, functions, and vocabulary, to the process, that is 'to use English to learn it' rather than 'to learn to use English'. This brings us to the next model of learning, Task-Based Learning.

ACTIVITY 4

Look at these typical CLT-related problems and think of possible solutions that you could use with your learners.

1 Learners are shy about working in pairs or groups.
2 The class is very large and the seats and desks cannot be moved.
3 The class has to prepare for written, not spoken, exams.
4 Learners often ask for new vocabulary in English which you are unprepared for.

Task-Based Learning

Task-Based Learning (TBL) focuses on the 'process' of communicating by setting learners tasks to complete using the target language. During this process, it is claimed, the learners **acquire** language as they try to express themselves and understand others. The tasks can range from **information gap** to problem-solving tasks. One advantage of TBL is that learners are given the opportunity to use the full range of skills and language they have at the same time, rather than in discrete units, as they sometimes do with the CLT model.

A typical task sequence may include:

– pre-tasks: these are activities which prepare learners to complete a task, for example, by guiding learners through an example of the task they will have to do. There can be a number of pre-tasks in one lesson.
– tasks: these form the main body of the lesson and can involve a number of steps. For example, learners working in pairs or groups may first complete the task, then prepare a report on the task, and finally present the report to the class.
– post-tasks: these move away from activities designed to promote fluency to those designed to promote accuracy.

An example of a task might be to plan a journey by train. The class is divided into groups of five. Each learner in the group has information which the rest of the learners need, for example, train times, the route, the price of tickets, etc. By sharing this information the group can successfully plan the trip and in doing so consolidate and extend their language ability.

There are several uncertainties regarding TBL. What language the learners acquire depends on how the task is performed, so it is difficult to state what language will be learnt, if any – the learners may avoid learning or using new language and make do with the language they have. Learners may also feel that they are not 'learning' or 'being taught' as there is no formal input or practice stage. As with CLT, some learners feel that interacting with L2 speakers rather than the teacher is a waste of time.

PORTFOLIO ACTIVITY

Plan a task you could use with your learners. What language do you think they will need to complete the task? Try out the activity with your class. Make a note of the language they use and any language that they acquire.

What was the outcome of the lesson? Did your learners learn anything or develop any of their language skills? If so, what? Will you use tasks in the future?

Summary

Teaching has been influenced by a wide variety of methods and trends. New methods have been introduced as part of the ongoing search for the 'best' way to teach. In some ways this has been beneficial – we now know a lot more about teaching and learning than we did 50 years ago, and the learner's role has been integrated into the learning and teaching process. However, some ways of teaching that might still be useful – translation, using a situation to demonstrate meaning, and drilling, to take three examples – have been sidelined. At the same time, teachers have constantly had to keep up with the latest trends which may or may not be appropriate for them or their learners.

We are now at the point where there is more emphasis on teachers and learners making their own choices about how to teach and learn. Teachers can use the back-catalogue of methods as a starting point to make decisions about this process.

Case study

Go to the 'Case study' section at the back of the book and listen to a teacher talk about their experiences of teaching methods.

3 LANGUAGE

In this chapter we explore:

– what language is
– how we use language to **interact**
– language in the classroom.

Language

Language is a tool we use to communicate with other people. We **encode** what we want to say using language which is made up of a range of components. One way of looking at language is to start with the smallest component and work upwards:

– individual letters and sounds, for example, 'c' and /k/
– combined letters and sounds, for example, 'th' – /θ/ ('think') or /ð/ ('the')
– words – 'cat', /kæt/
– phrases – 'the happy cat' (**noun phrase**), 'sat down' (**verb phrase**)
– clauses – 'the happy cat sat down'
– sentences – 'The happy cat sat down on the muddy mat.'

The individual sounds of a spoken language are called **phonemes**. There are two types of phoneme: **vowels**, for example, the /æ/ sound in 'c<u>a</u>t', and **consonants**, for example, the /k/ sound in '<u>c</u>at'. As we can see, the letter is not always the same as the symbol that represents the sound. Also, there are a lot more vowel and consonant sounds, 44, compared with the number of letters in the English alphabet – 26. See the phonetic chart on page 29.

The particular vowels and consonants we need to produce when we speak are often different or do not exist in other languages. For example:

– the 'i' phonemes in English, the /ɪ/ in 'ship', and /i:/ in 'sheep', do not exist in Italian
– Spanish speakers sometimes have problems with the /b/ in 'ban' and the /v/ in 'van' since these are not distinctly separate phonemes in Spanish
– to Japanese speakers /æ/ (cat) and /ʌ/ (cut) can sound similar as the Japanese 'a' sound is about half way between the two.

Teachers need to be aware of their learners' weak areas and give them practice in recognizing and producing these sounds correctly.

Vowels and consonants can combine in a number of ways. For example, we can have a vowel + vowel (**thea**tre); consonant + vowel (**pe**ncil); consonant + consonant (**br**eak). As with phonemes, there are some combinations of letters in English that can cause problems for speakers of other languages. So, for example, Italian speakers tend to add an extra vowel to some final consonants such as bi**g**, or lea**d**. Greek speakers may find the consonant clusters /nk/ (thi**nk**) or /mp/ (ju**mp**) difficult to pronounce.

ACTIVITY 1

Look at the list of words below and at the underlined phonemes. Do these sounds exist in your language? Can you think of any other sounds that exist in English that do not exist in your language? Are there any sounds in your language that do not exist in English?

<u>th</u>at   <u>w</u>indow   ha<u>v</u>e   c<u>ou</u>ld   <u>sh</u>oe   ri<u>c</u>e   <u>ch</u>eck   si<u>ng</u>   f<u>oo</u>t   m<u>ea</u>t

---

As you can see from the above, English spelling is only loosely connected to the actual sound of the words. English is not a **phonetic language**. If we are reading something, we need to be able to interpret the written form correctly, for example, the word 'tough' is pronounced /tʌf/. Other words with the same 'ough' spelling could be pronounced /aʊ/ 'bough', /ɔ:/ 'bought', or /əʊ/ 'dough'. If we are listening to something and want to write it down, we need to able to spell what we hear correctly. For example, the sound /aɪ/ can be spelt using 'i' ('five') or 'y' (eye). Some words are spelt differently but sound the same (**homophones**), for example 'mail' and 'male' – /meɪl/.

ACTIVITY 2

Using the chart on the next page as a guide, match the words on the left to the correct phonetic representations on the right.

classroom	/bʊk/
desk	/lɪsn/
student	/klɑːsruːm/
listen	/desk/
blackboard	/tiːtʃə/
pencil	/pensl/
teacher	/blækbɔːd/
book	/stjuːdnt/

We put individual letters or sounds together to form words. For example, 'classroom' is made up of the following letters and sounds:

c l a s s r o o m   /ˈk l ɑː s r uː m/

Figure 3.1   *The* **phonetic chart** *(from* New English File Pre-Intermediate*)*

'Classroom' has two **syllables** – 'class' + 'room'. Syllables are made up of a vowel or a vowel + consonant combination. When a word has more than one syllable, one syllable is emphasized more than another. So, for example, in the words 'table', '**mo**ther', and '**doc**tor', the first syllable is emphasized or stressed. In the words 'be**lief**', 'at**tack**', and 'cas**sette**', the second syllable is stressed.

Word **stress** can be indicated in the phonetic transcription of a word with a / ˈ / symbol before the stressed syllable, for example, 'table' – / ˈteɪbl/, 'cassette' – /kəˈset/. Often the **unstressed** vowel, called the **schwa**, is pronounced as /ə/ as in /kəˈset/.

The meaning of a word can change with the stress, for example, '**con**tract' (noun, a document), 'con**tract**' (verb, to get smaller). Quite often nouns have the first syllable stress and verbs have the second syllable. However, there are no straightforward rules for word stress in English.

Words can be categorized as **synonyms**, words which have the same or a similar meaning, for example, 'cut' and 'slice', or as opposites or **antonyms**, for example, 'big' and 'small'. However, words can be only labelled synonyms or antonyms in a limited way. We could say 'I cut the bread.' and 'I sliced the bread', but 'I cut my thumb.' and 'I sliced my thumb' have different meanings.

ACTIVITY 3

Underline the stressed syllable in these words. Use a dictionary if necessary.

classroom   telephone   important   computer   explain
example   instructions exercise   conversation

An important feature of English **pronunciation** is the way in which individual words often flow into each other without a clear break. This is particularly true when a consonant at the end of a word meets a vowel at the beginning of the next, for example:

It's **in** another area.   /ɪtsɪnænʌðɜːreərɪə/

This often makes listening difficult for learners and practice is needed to get used to the various ways that words **link** together. See 'Listening', page 48.

In spoken English we don't stress every word equally. We say some words more clearly and strongly. These are usually the content words, i.e. the words that carry important information, such as nouns and verbs, rather than the words we use to link the content words together (see 'Word types', page 31). In the sentences below the key words are shown in bold. These words are the ones that would normally be stressed:

Open your **books** on page **ten**.
Today we're going to **hear** a **story** about a **clown**.

Sentence stress can also change the meaning of a sentence. For example:

I love you.
I **love** you.
I love **you**.

ACTIVITY 4

Which question matches which sentence above?

Who do you love?
Who loves me?
What do you feel about me?

Often when we are speaking we want to focus on one piece of key information. Look at the example below in which the stressed word is shown in italics:

A I'll meet you in the staff room next Friday as usual.

B No, we'll have to meet in the staff room on *Thursday*. I'm off on Friday.

Here Speaker B is putting most stress on the day as it is the most important piece of information and it's necessary to show that it is different to what Speaker A is thinking or saying. This is called contrastive stress.

Intonation helps the listener to know if the speaker has finished (a fall) or not (a rise), for example:

I've been to Kenya.

compared with

I've been to Kenya, South Africa, Ethiopia …

Intonation can also indicate that the speaker is asking something, for example, 'Finished?' or stating something – 'Finished.'

A speaker's use of stress and intonation, and also volume and pitch, can also tell us about how they feel – excited, angry, positive, tired, etc.

Word types

Words work in different ways. For example, some words refer to people, things, actions, or ideas, for example, 'teacher', 'board', 'write', 'education'. Other words are used to help put sentences together, for example, 'if', 'and', 'then', 'the', 'about'. Other words tell us about an action or event, for example, 'slowly', 'beautifully', 'suddenly', or about things and people, for example, 'light', happy', 'useful'. Here is a list of word types.

Word type (or part of speech)	Example	Description
verb	know, own	state verb, refers to unchanging conditions
verb	read (a book)	dynamic verb, refers to actions; can have an object (**transitive**)
verb	laugh	dynamic verb, refers to actions; cannot have a direct object (**intransitive**)
noun	book driver beauty	refers to things, people, ideas

Word type (or part of speech)	Example	Description
adjective	small	describes things, people, and ideas
adverb	slowly today here	tells us about an action or state in terms of how, when, or where
pronoun	I, me, my, mine who	replaces nouns and refers to people, places, or things
conjunction	and, but, or	joins words, phrases, or sentences
preposition	in, at, on	used before a noun to show place, position, time, or method

We change word endings and beginnings for a wide range of reasons. Here are some examples:

adjective ⟶ noun		happy ⟶ happ*iness* [**suffix**]
adjective ⟶ adverb		quick ⟶ quick*ly*
noun ⟶ adjective		fog ⟶ fog*gy*
		comfort ⟶ comfort*able*
verb ⟶ noun		listen ⟶ listen*er*
		explain ⟶ expla*nation*
adjective ⟶ opposite		economical ⟶ *un*economical [**prefix**]
verb ⟶ opposite		agree ⟶ *dis*agree
-er	comparing	tall ⟶ tall*er*
-est	superlative	big ⟶ big*gest*
's	possessive	Hana*'s* flowers
-s	plural	cat ⟶ cat*s*
	irregular plural	mouse ⟶ *mice*
-(e)s	3rd person singular	He go*es* to work by bicycle.
-ed	regular past simple	The course *finished* last week.
	irregular past simple	I *went* to town.
	past participle	They are *packed* in boxes.
	irregular past participle	They were *seen* in a club.
-ing	present participle	They're *reading*.
	gerund	They like *reading*.

ACTIVITY 5

Complete the following table by changing or adding to the word endings and word beginnings. Where no word exists there is a line in the box.

Verb	Noun	Adjective	Opposite (of adjective)
employ		employed	
	belief		unbelievable
–		happy	
–	possibility		
	education		
direct		direct	
comfort		comfortable	

We can put words into groups that belong to the same category. These are sometimes called lexical sets, for example, we can make a group under the heading 'living things':

Living things → plants
                animals → mammals → four-legged
                                            two-legged → humans

Phrases
Words come together to form noun phrases, for example, 'the bus stop', 'an old shoe', and verb phrases, for example, 'get on with', 'he has been writing'. Some words often come together or **collocate**, for example:

'make a plan' (not 'do a plan'*)   'fast food' (not 'quick food')
'do a good job' (not 'make a good job'*)   'a close shave' (but not 'a far shave')

In a noun phrase, the adjective goes before the noun, for example, 'a blue book'. However, the order of words in a phrase is different in other languages. For example, in French the order is reversed and the noun comes before the adjective – 'le livre bleu'.

In verb phrases, different combinations of verbs and word endings are used to refer to different times and periods, for example:

now   I am writing a book.
past   I wrote a book.
future   I am going to write a book. OR I'll write a book.

past till now   I've been writing this book for six months.
past experience I've read this book twice.

We use other **structures** to refer to facts, possibility, our feeling or view about something. They are relatively fixed patterns of words which can be adapted to fit what we want to say. For example:

Structure	Example	Function
present simple	I *write* books.	state a fact
if + present simple + 'will'	*If* I leave now, I'*ll* arrive on time.	talk about a possible future
should + main verb	You *should see* a doctor.	give advice
might + main verb	It *might be* sunny tomorrow.	speculate about the future

ACTIVITY 6

Match the description of the structures with the sentences on the right and describe the function.

Structure	Example	Function
Present continuous	I *have cleaned* the blackboard.	
Present simple of 'to be'	When I saw him he *had grown* a beard.	
Past simple of 'to be'	Please *put* the book on the table.	
Infinitive	My name *is* Mario.	
Present perfect	His teacher *was* very strict.	
Past perfect	He *is writing* a letter at the moment.	

There are two types of verb phrase which combine a verb, noun, and particle (e.g. 'off', 'after'). They differ in the possible combination and order of the three elements. The phrases with the asterisk indicate that the word order is incorrect.

Type A
turn off the radio
turn the radio off
turn it off
*turn off it

Type B
look after her mother
*look her mother after
*look her after
look after her

ACTIVITY 7

Look at the scrambled phrases below and put them into the correct order. Can you identify which of the two types of verb phrase they are?

get of way out the	throw the away rubbish
going him she is out with	take shoes your off

Clauses

Clauses are the next building blocks which we use to put sentences together. A clause is a group of words that includes a subject and a verb, for example, 'the friend who visited last weekend'. Clauses can be combined to form sentences, for example, 'Lucy is the friend who visited last weekend.' The standard word order in English is subject + verb + object, for example, 'I saw the child'. However, this is different in other languages. In German, for example, the verb often goes at the end of the sentence. In Japanese, the pronoun would probably not be used and the word order would be 'Child (object) saw.'

The word order in English determines whether a sentence is a statement (subject + verb + object) or a question (auxiliary verb + subject + verb + object), for example, 'Did you see the child?'

ACTIVITY 8

How many clauses can you identify in these sentences?

The train which has just arrived at platform one is out of service.

Unless there is a shop in the village where they live, people who live in the countryside have to take the bus or drive to a supermarket to do their shopping.

When we put sentences together we need to think about the relationship between the words, for example:

I've got *an* English–English *dictionary*.	'dictionary' is singular so 'an'. We use 'an' rather than 'a' because it is followed by 'English' which starts with a vowel.
They've got *some friends* in Brazil.	'Friends' is plural so we use 'some'.

Longer texts

Longer stretches of language, for example, a series of sentences should be logically organized and signposted with words indicating the relationship between the parts of the text ('then', 'after that', 'next', etc.). The line of argument or the sequence of events should follow a particular order that makes sense to the reader. For example:

> First, take the wheel off the frame. OK. Now, take the tyre off the rim. Got it. Good. Next, put the tyre in a bowl of water.

> The bus stopped suddenly so I slammed on the brakes. Then the car behind me hit the back of my car.

> When I was young I lived abroad and came home to Brazil in 2002. After that I stayed with my family in São Paulo. Now I'm living on my own in a flat downtown.

There is more information about longer texts in chapter 7 from page 88 onwards.

Longer stretches of language which occur when people interact also contain relationships between words and ideas which we will look at in the next section.

Using language to interact

We interact with different people for different reasons in different situations in different ways. For example, if we want a family member to close a door we might just shout 'Door!' If we were with someone we didn't know and wanted them to shut a door, we probably wouldn't just shout 'Door' but use a more formal and polite expression.

There is a wide range of expressions that perform certain 'functions', i.e. the things we do with language, for example, there are general functions such as thanking, asking for information, inviting, suggesting, greeting, agreeing, and so on. Every function has **exponents**, i.e. fixed expressions which we use to perform the function. Some functions, for example, making a request, have a very wide range of exponents, for example, 'Could you …?', 'Would you mind …?', '…, please', 'I wonder if you could …', and so on.

There is also a group of expressions that we use to control the interaction between ourselves and the other speaker or speakers, for example, 'Could you say that again?', 'Can I just say …?'

ACTIVITY 9

Match the expression with the function. For example, 'Do you know what I mean?' is a way of checking if the other person understands you. Which are general functions and which are interactional functions?

Expression	Function
Do you know what I mean?	interrupting
Could you pass me that book?	asking for repetition
What do you think?	expressing our opinions
I'm not sure I agree.	checking that we have understood someone
Can I just say …?	apologizing
I'm really sorry.	*checking that someone understands you*
Do you mean…?	disagreeing
I don't think it should be allowed.	asking for other people's opinions
You can switch it on here.	giving instructions/information
Sorry, I didn't catch that.	asking someone to do something

Language users need to make choices about the language they choose to communicate with. This choice is very limited in the early stages of learning a language. For example, when beginners make a request, they might start by just using the names of things, like 'Milk', then a more complex phrase using '…, please.' , then 'Could I …?', 'Would you mind if I …?', etc. As their bank of language develops, the more choice they have and the more they can fine tune their message to fit the situation, what they want to say, the person or people they are talking to, and so on.

In some languages, the relationship between the speaker and listener is reflected in the grammar, for example, the use of 'you' in French – 'vous' for more formal situations and 'tu' for less formal situations. In other languages, the relationship is reflected in the verb ending, for example, in Japanese 'there is' can be 'aru' (short, informal) or 'arimasu' (long, formal). English does not make the grammatical distinction between the different forms of 'you' or short/long verb forms, but there are certain forms that are more or less informal as we saw with the 'Door!' example. There are no rules but generally speaking the longer phrase is the more polite, for example, 'Bank?', 'Where is the bank?', 'Excuse me, could you tell me where the bank is, please?'

As speakers, what we say has to fit what the previous person has said. For example, if someone says, 'If I had lots of money, I'd love to go to Jamaica.'

we might reply 'So would I'. To be able to make this kind of response we need to be able to do several things, i.e. replace what the first speaker said with 'So' (= I would go to Jamaica if I had lots of money), add 'would' to fit the 'if' and 'I' to change the subject. We also saw in 'Sentence stress' on page 30 that what we say and how we say it depends to some extent on what the previous speaker said, for example, 'Who do you love?' – 'I love **you**.'

ACTIVITY 10

Put the sentences in the scrambled telephone conversation below into the correct order. How did you know what order they went in? Look at the ways in which the speakers interact and respond to each other. You have been given the first two sentences.

A Hello, Bangor 35363.

B Oh hello, can I speak to Martin, please?

Goodbye.

I'm not sure, but I think he has a meeting at two o'clock so he'll be back before then.

Oh, OK. Do you know when he will be back?

I'm afraid I have to go out at that time. Will you tell him I called?

I'm sorry, but he's not in at the moment.

Thank you. Goodbye.

The surname's Jonson.

Certainly. Could I have your name?

Sorry, I didn't catch your surname. John …?

Is that J-O-H-N-S-O-N?

So that's J-O-N. Fine. I'll tell him you rang.

It's actually without the 'h'.

It's John Jonson. He should have my number.

Language in the classroom

We can divide language activities in the classroom into two categories – introducing language and using language that has already been encountered. As learners progress, they will constantly meet language for the first time, sometimes inside the classroom, sometimes outside. At this point they need to know what this language means or refers to. They also need to know how to form it – how to spell it, pronounce it, its relationship to other words, the word endings, and so on. Finally they need to be able to use it to communicate, either in spoken or written form, and to understand it when it is used by other people.

Meaning

There are many ways of helping learners understand the meaning of a word or phrase. For example, with a word like 'job' we can:

– translate the word from English into the L1
– give the learners examples of types of jobs, for example, by providing pictures of people doing different jobs
– provide an explanation or definition in English
– tell the learners to look up the word either in a monolingual or bilingual dictionary
– give them example sentences using 'job'.

The learners also need to know the meaning of similar words, for example, 'work' and how they are used. Both refer to something that we do to earn money, but 'job' suggests something that is more regular. They can both be nouns, but 'job' is countable – 'I've got a part-time job.' and 'work' is uncountable – 'I've got some part-time work.' (not 'a part-time work'*). It takes time for learners to understand these similarities and differences and it is important to give them plenty of clear examples to develop this understanding.

For a structure we need to provide a context which illustrates the meaning clearly. For example, to explain one meaning of the past continuous we could give the context of someone talking about something they did in the past and the background to that event or action (see Figure 3.2).

We can help learners understand the meaning with the use of visual representations. For example, to understand how we refer to time we can use **time lines** (see Figure 3.3). 'Now' refers to the time of the utterance (when the person speaks).

A time line can be used in several ways. The teacher can draw one on the board and give an explanation. Alternatively the learners could be given an example sentence and asked to design an appropriate time line. Another way would be for the teacher to draw a time line without an example sentence and ask the class to supply a suitable one.

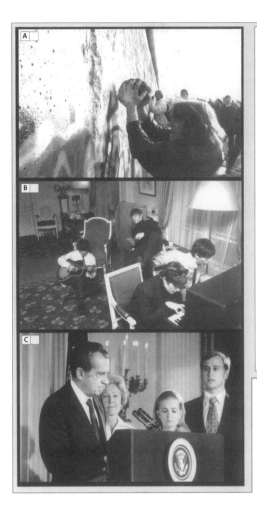

HARRY BENSON spent 50 years taking dramatic and memorable photographs for national newspapers and magazines. Here he talks about three of his best-known pictures.

1 I took this picture on August 9th 1974. He was saying goodbye to his cabinet and the White House staff after the 'Watergate' scandal. All his family were standing round him. You can see from their faces what they were feeling.

2 In 1989, I was working in London on a story when suddenly I heard the news that the Russians were planning to make Berlin an open city. So I got on a plane. When I arrived in Berlin many people, young and old, were attacking the wall with stones. The woman in the photo was shouting, 'I hate it, I hate it'.

3 When I took this photo we were in a hotel room in Paris in 1964. John and Paul were at the piano and at first nothing much was happening, but suddenly they became completely focused. First the melody came, and then the words. *'Baby's good to me you know, she's happy as can be you know…'.* They were composing their song *I feel fine*.

Figure 3.2   An example of providing a context to illustrate meaning (from New English File Pre-intermediate*)*

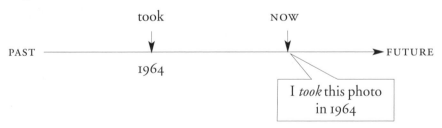

Figure 3.3   Time line referring to an event in the past (past simple)

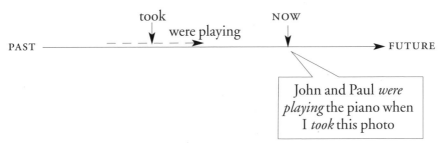

Figure 3.4 Referring to a past event (past simple) and the background to the event (past continuous)

ACTIVITY 11

Design time lines for the present perfect with 'since' and the past simple with 'for'.

It is important to check that the learners understand the meaning of the language they are studying. This can often be done by monitoring the learners' use of the language in spoken or written activities. Another way is to use **concept questions**. For example, to check the use of the present simple to talk about a scheduled event in the future we need to check that the learners understand whether the sentences refer to the past, present, or future and what sort of events are being referred to:

The flight from Dubai arrives at seven o'clock this evening.
The bus leaves in ten minutes.

Do the sentences refer to an event in the present or future? (the future)
Where does the information come from? (from a timetable or schedule)
Can the speaker change the information? (no)
Which tense is used in both sentences? (the present simple)

Another way of helping learners to understand the meaning of a structure is to provide a background situation. The situation can be introduced in a variety of ways including using pictures, a dialogue, a short text, and real objects. For example, 'going to' + verb to predict an event can be introduced through illustrations of situations in which there are clues of the likely future event, see Figure 3.5.

Figure 3.5 Using a situation to illustrate meaning (from Open Doors 1*)*

Form

Learners need to know the form the language takes, both spoken and written. In the case of the past continuous, the form is the past simple of 'be' ('was, 'were') and the verb + 'ing'. When it is spoken the 'e' in 'was' is often not stressed and the 's' pronounced as /z/, i.e. /wəz/. 'Be' changes according to the person or persons referred to, i.e. 'I was talking', 'They were standing'. We should also include details about the question and negative forms.

For vocabulary items like 'job' learners need to know which words it collocates with, for example, verb phrases such as 'get a job', 'do a good job', and noun phrases such as 'job application', and 'job description'. It is important to give learners full-sentence examples so that they can see how the word fits into the overall sentence pattern. Learners also need to know how to pronounce the word. In this case it is straightforward, /dʒɒb/.

Use

We use the past continuous to provide the background to an event or action, for example, when we are telling a story. The event or action is described using the past simple. We can refer to either the background or event first, i.e. 'I took this picture … He was saying …' or 'I was working in London … suddenly heard the news …'

For vocabulary, learners need to know the limits of the use of a word. For 'job' we can only use it as a noun whereas 'work' can also be a verb – 'I work in an office.' 'What do you do?' is more commonly used than 'What's your job?' to ask someone about their employment.

Some classroom ideas for use in the case of 'job', the past continuous, and 'going to' to make predictions are:

– get the class to design a questionnaire about jobs people do, what they want to do in the future, and so on
– get the class to mime situations where there is a background and an event, for example, someone is taking a bath and the doorbell rings
– get the class to make their own illustrations, for example, a glass about to be knocked over, an acrobat losing his balance on a high wire.

Using the language, both in spoken and written form, is described in detail in chapters 5 and 7.

ACTIVITY 12

The verbs 'go', 'do', and 'play' are used to refer to sports or leisure activities:

play	tennis, football, golf, basketball, rugby, baseball, billiards
go	jogging, hiking, walking, running, fishing, skiing
do	karate, aerobics, tai chi

What are the differences between the three verbs and how would you help learners understand these differences?

ACTIVITY 13

A typical situation with a class in the middle of a course or term is that the learners have covered certain areas of the language but have yet to fully understand all aspects of the meaning, form, and use.

For example, a lower intermediate class know about the past simple and can form verbs using '-ed' but still make some mistakes with the pronunciation and are not sure of some irregular verbs. They can form questions in the past but are not sure about questions with 'did'. They can talk about leisure activities but confuse 'play', 'go', and 'do' verb phrases.

Imagine you are the teacher. You have a recorded conversation of two people talking about what they did last weekend. The conversation contains:

– a range of question forms
– verbs in the past simple, both regular and irregular
– use of prepositions to talk about location and time
– vocabulary to do with leisure activities.

You can listen to the conversation on the CD (in this pack) and read the script on page 179. Decide the language aims and how to achieve these aims using the conversation and a sequence of activities.

See chapter 8 for more discussion about planning a lesson.

Summary

It is important for the language teacher to know as much as possible about the language that they are teaching. The language system is complex and learners need to be guided through it. They will often come across language for the first time which they will need to incorporate into their own language system. To do this they need to know what it means, what form it takes, and how to use it. To help them with this process teachers need to choose the most appropriate texts and activities and give learners the opportunity they need to input language, use it, and modify their understanding of that language until they are able to recall and use it automatically.

Case study

Go to the 'Case study' section at the back of the book and listen to a teacher talk about their experiences of teaching language.

4 LISTENING

In this chapter we explore:

– the listening process
– listening skills
– listening in the classroom.

The listening process

We listen to a wide variety of things, for example:

– what someone says during a conversation – face to face or on the telephone
– announcements giving information, for example, at an airport or railway station
– the weather forecast on the radio
– a play on the radio
– music
– someone else's conversation (eavesdropping)
– a lecture
– professional advice, for example, at the doctor's, in the bank
– instructions, for example, on how to use a photocopier or other machinery
– directions
– a taped dialogue in class.

What we listen to comes from a variety of sources, for example, other people, radio, TV, CD, video, DVD, cassette, the Internet, and the telephone. The length of what we listen to varies greatly, for example, a train announcement or a play on the radio.

ACTIVITY 1

Can you add any more items to the list of things we listen to? How long is each example? How do you think this might affect the way we listen?

We listen for a purpose, but this purpose can be very different depending on the situation:

– listening for specific details
– listening for general meaning

– listening for the general idea or **gist**.

There is also a difference between listening:

– for information
– for enjoyment or social reasons
– to learn new language.

For example, if you listen to a friend giving you instructions about how to get to their new home, you would want to listen carefully to *all* the details, and possibly note them down. If you are listening to a friend talking about their holiday, you would listen 'normally', i.e. you would listen for the general meaning, probably focusing on anything of particular interest. In contrast, if you were listening to a radio play, you would probably be listening for enjoyment, and for a general idea of what the play is about. We would not expect to remember all the details of the play or focus on particular information. These different kinds of listening are similar for all ages. If children are being told how to make something, for example, a puppet, they have to listen to everything they are told. If they are listening to someone telling a story, they will be listening for gist and enjoyment.

For learners, listening is how spoken language becomes input, i.e. it is the first stage of learning new language. In the classroom this happens through listening to the teacher, listening to a CD or tape or watching a video, and listening to other learners.

ACTIVITY 2

Look back at the list on page 45 of what we listen to. In each situation would you be listening for:

– specific details, for general meaning, or for gist?
– information, enjoyment, or language input?

Listening is a receptive skill, i.e. we receive language rather than produce it. Listening is the process of interpreting messages – what people say. We saw in chapter 3 that language involves putting messages into a form that other people can understand using these elements:

– individual sounds
– syllables
– words which may be linked together with some sounds being dropped or changed
– phrases
– clauses
– grammatical structures
– sentences
– longer stretches of spoken English.

Intonation, and word and sentence stress, also add meaning. Listeners also have to deal with speakers repeating themselves, making **false starts**, pauses, and noises ('ums' and 'ahs') . The listener has to be able to **decode** all of this as quickly as the speaker produces it. This obviously takes a huge amount of practice.

Even though listening is a receptive skill it is not necessarily a passive one. A listener can either be **active** or **passive**. When we are in a conversation we listen, respond appropriately, and sometimes stop the conversation to ask the speaker to repeat what they said, to slow down, or to clarify what they have said, or to interrupt. This is active listening – the listener has some control of what they are listening to. There are also times when listening is more passive and we do not have to respond, for example, when we listen to the news on the radio or a public announcement.

ACTIVITY 3

Look back at the list on page 45 of what we listen to. In each situation do we listen actively or passively?

Listening skills

Learners need to develop the following skills:

– learning to listen in various ways
– adapting the way they listen according to the text and the reason for
  listening
– recognizing the features of spoken English
– using visual and textual clues to help them
– listening actively – asking for repetition, clarification, etc.
– developing their background knowledge.

As we have seen, we listen in different ways depending on what we are listening to and why. Learners also need to develop this skill. At the same time, they should use the clues they have around them to help them understand what someone is saying.

As well as developing their vocabulary and grammatical knowledge, learners need to develop their understanding of pronunciation (see 'Language' pages 27–30). For example, if a learner knows that consonants and vowels link together, for example, 'an old apple' – /ænəʊldæpl/, or that the first syllable in 'telephone' is stressed and the second 'e' is unstressed and is pronounced /ə/, and the final 'e' is not pronounced at all, they will be more likely to understand than a learner who expects each word to be pronounced separately or for the three 'e's in 'telephone' to be pronounced in the same way.

Learners need to develop the confidence to control a conversation by asking the person speaking to speak more slowly, explain what they have said, repeat something, and so on. If not, they will lose the opportunity to learn and communicate successfully.

It is not just what people say but customs and social background that can become barriers to understanding. **Paralinguistic features** (gestures, hand movements, and facial expressions) can often be different from one country to another. For example, in Bulgaria a nod of the head means no, in Britain it means yes. Learners should learn as much as possible about the culture of the country and people they are going to communicate with.

Listening in the classroom

When we are practising listening in the classroom it is helpful to think about how we listen in real life. We should try to:

– ask learners to do things in class which they would be likely to do outside
– give them the information they would have in the real world, for example,
  about the context
– give them the opportunity to listen actively

– give them the opportunity to listen in different ways, i.e. for specific details, for gist, and so on
– give learners the opportunity to listen to a range of situations, accents, and topics.

There are two basic types of material – authentic and invented. For example, a taped dialogue of two actors in a studio reading out a script is less authentic. A video of two people in a real situation, for example, at home or in a shop, and talking without a script is more authentic. Generally we need to use more carefully adapted texts, and therefore less authentic texts, at lower levels and gradually introduce more authentic speech as the learners develop. When we do use more authentic material at lower levels we can make the task that we ask learners to do easier. For example, if we ask our learners to listen to a discussion we could simply ask them whether the speakers agree. At a higher level we would ask more detailed questions – what do they disagree about? why? and so on.

Listening activities can be planned in three stages:

– **pre-listening** – activities which help your learners prepare for what they will hear
– **listening** – activities which are usually a type of task, for example, filling in a chart, answering questions, following a route on a map, making notes, etc.
– **post-listening** – activities which are a chance to check learners' understanding of what they have been listening to, give feedback, and consolidate what they have learnt.

Pre-listening stage

Pre-listening activities should help learners by focusing their attention on the topic, activating any knowledge they have about the topic, and making it clear to the learners what they have to do while they listen, for example:

– discussing the topic or type of conversation with the learners
– helping the learners to develop their vocabulary related to the topic
– giving learners information about the context, for example, who is talking, where they are
– getting the learners to predict what they will hear
– making sure learners understand what they have to do while they are listening, i.e. do they have to do something, write something, draw something, and so on? If you are giving them some comprehension questions to answer, they need to read them and check they understand them before they hear the text.
– make sure they understand why they are doing the activity, for example, to introduce new language, to practise listening to native speakers, etc.

ACTIVITY 4

Here are five examples of listening texts (a–e), followed by five examples of pre-listening activities (1–5). Match the texts with the activities.

    a someone talking about their family
    b an automatic message about banking facilities
    c a TV programme about the environment
    d a radio programme about education in the UK
    e someone talking about their job.

1 Before you listen note down things:

    – you would like to know about schools in Britain, for example, do all children in British schools have to learn a foreign language?
    – you know about schools in Britain, for example, children in Britain start school at the age of five.

2 Do you agree or disagree with these statements?

    – There are too many cars on the roads.
    – Nuclear fuel is better for the environment than coal or oil.

3 Match the words with the definitions:

account	to borrow money for a certain period of time
balance	to move money from one place to another
transfer	where a customer's money is kept
loan	how much money a customer has in their account

4 Note down as many words for relatives (brother, sister, uncle, and so on) as you can. Here is a chart you can use:

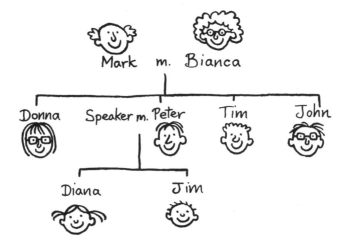

Figure 4.1 A family tree (from Presenting New Language)

5   Think of three jobs. What are the good and the bad aspects of each job?

You could consider the following questions:
- Does the job have long hours?
- Does the job have long holidays?
- Is it stressful?
- Is it boring?
- Is it well paid?

Listening stage

While pre-listening activities are about preparing for the questions or a task, listening activities are about the learners finding the answers or doing the task. There are various types of activities, for example:

- answering questions – comprehension, multiple choice, true or false
- completing something – a form, grid, chart, picture, etc. using information that learners hear
- following directions on a map
- matching what is being said with a set of pictures
- doing something in response to what learners hear, for example, draw something, move in a certain way (stand up, sit down).

So, for example, in one of the pre-listening activities on page 50 the learners were asked two questions about the environment. In the listening stage they could gist listen to find out if the TV programme generally supports their view. They could then listen again and make a note of the details either for or against their view.

Some listening activities require learners to listen to a text and answer questions, while other activities require more interaction, i.e. learners listen then respond or react.

listen $\longrightarrow$ respond/react $\longrightarrow$ listen $\longrightarrow$ respond/react $\longrightarrow$
listen $\longrightarrow$ respond/react ...

We go through this process when, for example, we are following instructions. See 'Listen and physically respond' on pages 52 and 53.

To encourage active listening the learners should be given the chance to ask for clarification, repetition, check they have understood, and so on.

listen $\longrightarrow$ ask for repetition $\longrightarrow$ listen $\longrightarrow$ ask for clarification $\longrightarrow$
listen $\longrightarrow$ ...

Here are some examples of listening activities:

Listen and draw

Describe a room to your learners, for example, where the tables, chairs and other furniture are, how many windows and doors there are, and so on. Tell your learners to draw the room as you describe it.

Listen and match

The learners have a number of pictures of different people. You describe each of these people and the learners have to identify the correct picture.

Listen and order pictures or a dialogue

The learners have a number of pictures from a strip cartoon or story. They listen to the story and they have to put the pictures into the right order.

Listen and follow a route on a map

Learners listen to directions from point A to point B and they mark the route on a map.

Listen and complete a form

The learners have application forms which they complete according to what they hear, for example, someone giving their name and address, date of birth, work experience, and so on.

Listen and correct

The learners have a written text with details about a holiday. They hear someone describing the holiday but with a number of factual errors. Learners have to identify the errors.

Listen and physically respond

This is often known as Total Physical Response (TPR). Ask your learners to stand up if, for example, their name has an 'a' in it, they're wearing a T-shirt, their birthday is in May, and so on.

Another good example of TPR is the game 'Simon Says'. You can use this game to help learners practise careful listening, vocabulary for parts of the body, or just as an energizer in the middle of a lesson. In this game, learners must only respond to the command given if it is preceded by 'Simon says'. If the words 'Simon says' are left out, then learners should not obey the command, and anyone who does is out of the game. The learners must respond quickly and correctly.

Here is an example:

TEACHER Simon says put your hands on your head.
          (Learners do the action)
TEACHER Simon says touch your toes.
          (Learners do the action)
TEACHER Put your hands on your hips.
          (Learners should not respond)

This type of activity often appeals in particular to children because it is fun and competitive. Keeping lessons lively and entertaining can be very motivating for younger learners.

ACTIVITY 5

Look at the list of listening texts from Activity 4 on page 50. Can you think of suitable listening tasks for each of them? For example, for activity a, you might give the learners a family tree to complete.

Post-listening stage

The first thing you need to do after the learners have carried out the listening activity is to check the answers. Learners can compare their answers with each other first. You can then check the answers with the whole class.

Checking answers can help you analyze the particular difficulties that the learners have had with the listening activity. You might need to give some feedback if you can see that learners are having problems with a particular sound, structure, or vocabulary item.

Post-listening activities often move on from listening practice to practising other skills. So, for example, after hearing about someone's job or family, learners might be asked to talk to each other about their own family or job, or they could be asked to write something about their own family or job. Here are some other post-listening activities.

Speaking activities

Learners can be asked to speak about the issues mentioned in the listening text. For example, after listening to a text about British education, you can ask learners to consider how British schools are different from their own schools. It is a good idea to put a list of the things learners might consider on the board, for example, uniform, class sizes, length of school day, subjects studied. This can make the discussion more focused. Similarly, after listening to an automatic message about banking facilities, learners might do a role play between a customer and a call-centre operator.

Writing activities

Learners can be asked to write about the subject they have heard about. For example, after hearing about someone's family or job, you can ask learners to write a paragraph about their own family or job. This kind of task can often be given as homework.

Pronunciation activities

One important thing to do after a listening activity is to consider why learners didn't understand something. Here are two common features of spoken English which might cause problems:

– unstressed vowels: words which can be easily understood when they are heard in isolation often sound quite different in a sentence. As we saw in chapter 3, a particularly common sound in English which sometimes causes problems for learners is the schwa which is written as /ə/ in phonetic script. This is the sound we hear in unstressed vowels. You can make your learners aware of this by asking them first to listen to the way the vowels are pronounced in words on their own, such as 'you', 'a', 'of', and 'was', and then in the sentences: 'Did *you* go?', 'It's *a* box *of* matches', and 'He *was* there'.

– connected speech: as we saw in chapter 3, page 30, English speech tends to run words together, for example, 'did you' in the sentence 'Did you go?'. Activity 6 shows how you can alert your learners to this feature of English speech by getting them to listen to words spoken slowly and individually and then spoken at a normal speed so that they sometimes link together.

ACTIVITY 6

Listen to the dialogue below spoken in artificially careful speech. You will then hear the same dialogue spoken in a more natural way. As you listen to the second version underline in your book the places where the vowels are unstressed and the places where words seem to run into each other.

> A   Do you want me to make the dinner?
> B   That'd be nice.
> A   OK. What have we got in the fridge?
> B   Not a lot really. There isn't any meat. But I've got some pasta, and there are some tomatoes in the cupboard. And there's some cheese in the fridge.
> A   OK. That'll do. I can make some fresh tomato sauce for the pasta.

Summary

In this chapter we saw that we listen to a wide variety of texts. We also saw that the listening texts we use in class can be more or less authentic, and that we can gradually introduce more authentic texts at lower levels if we grade the activities appropriately. Learners need to learn how to listen – actively or passively, for gist or detail, to gain information or for enjoyment – and how to decode what they hear by developing an understanding of the features of spoken English.

To help them with this process, teachers need to provide activities which give learners practice in these areas. These are usually organized in three integrated stages: pre-listening, listening, and post-listening.

Case study

Go to the 'Case study' section at the back of the book and listen to a teacher talk about their experiences of teaching listening.

5 SPEAKING

In this chapter we explore:

– the speaking process
– the differences between spoken and written language
– speaking skills
– speaking in the classroom.

The speaking process

We speak in many different types of situation. For example:

– talking to someone face to face
– talking to someone on the phone
– a learner answering a question in class
– someone giving a speech
– taking part in a meeting
– an **exchange** between a customer and an assistant in a shop
– asking a stranger for directions
– chatting to friends.

ACTIVITY 1

Can you think of any other situations we speak in?

We speak for many reasons – to be sociable, because we want something, because we want other people to do something, to do something for someone else, to respond to someone else, to express our feelings or opinion about something, to exchange information, to refer to an action or event in the past, present, or future, the possibility of something happening, and so on.

Speaking is a productive skill. It involves putting a message together, communicating the message, and interacting with other people. We put a message together using all the elements of the language described in chapter 3 but this time we are constructing rather than interpreting. As with listening, this is a complex task and learners need a lot of practice to develop this skill. To put together a message, for example, to ask somebody to send you an email, you could say:

Could you email me?

In spoken form it would sound like this:

/kədjuui:meɪlmi:/

'Email' is probably the most important word so it is given the most stress. All four words will link up and sound like one long word. The speaker's intonation will probably go up at the end of the sentence. The speaker has chosen 'Could you' from a range of possible forms we use to make requests, for example, 'Would you mind …?', 'I'd be grateful if you could …', and so on, to fit the situation and their relationship to the listener.

Interacting

Spoken interaction involves two or more people talking to each other, for example, one person makes a request and the other person responds. We call this an exchange, for example:

   A Could you email me?
   B Yes, of course.

We also use words and sounds to show that we are listening to someone and to indicate how we feel about what they are saying. For example:

Really?	Fine.
Really!	Mm.
I see.	Uh.
OK.	Oh!

ACTIVITY 2

Listen to the dialogue and check which words and sounds you hear. Is the second speaker enthusiastic or not?

Spoken and written language: some differences

In spoken English people do not always speak in full sentences, for example, 'Is it going to rain today?' – 'Could do.'. In this case we use the term **utterance** rather than sentence.

In written English people usually write complete sentences. Written English is organized into paragraphs, pages, chapters, and complete texts, for example, a book or an article in a magazine. Spoken English comes in the form of **turns** – one person's part in an exchange between two or more people.

Another difference is the way in which written language can be planned, whereas spoken language is often unplanned, unless you're giving a prepared speech or presentation.

When you speak you give clues through the use of stress, pauses, intonation, or gestures. When you write, all the information has to be on the page. Your reader cannot stop and ask you a question to make things clearer.

Spoken English is messy – when people speak they often repeat themselves, speak in incomplete sentences, hesitate and pause between words, and use **fillers** – short sounds or words that give us more time to think and put a message together. This is true in many if not all languages, not just English. Written English is much tidier and more organized.

ACTIVITY 3

Fill in the missing sections in the table.

Speaking	Writing
Not usually planned or prepared beforehand.	1
2	Sentences are carefully organized and accurate.
Stress, intonation, gestures, and facial expressions carry meaning.	3
4	Writing is linear, i.e. it goes in one direction without repetitions or revisions.

ACTIVITY 4

Listen to the two versions of a conversation. Which **fillers** do you notice in the second version?

Er ...	Kind of ...
What I mean is ...	How shall I put it ...
You know ...	The fact is...
Sort of ...	I mean ...
If you know what I mean ...	The thing is...

Similarities

There are also similarities between writing and speech. As we saw earlier, you speak differently depending on whom you are speaking to and why. Similarly, with written language, the type of writing varies depending on whom it is written for and why: a letter to a friend is written in a different way from a shopping list or an instruction manual about a car.

Speaking skills

Learners need to develop the following skills:

– producing **connected speech**
– the ability to interact
– talking round gaps in their knowledge
– speaking in a range of contexts
– balancing accuracy and fluency.

Learners need to develop their ability to string sounds and words together as we saw with /kədjuui:meɪlmi:/. As we have seen, they also need to interact successfully with other speakers – respond appropriately and use the appropriate language for the situation they are in and the person they are talking to. Especially in the early stages of their development, learners need to be able to 'talk round' words or expressions they don't know so that the conversation doesn't get stuck while they think of the right word. They need to learn expressions to define things, such as 'the thing we use for ...' Learners need to practise speaking in a wide range of contexts – with people they know, strangers, at work or school, in a shop or restaurant, and so on. Learners also need to be able to produce language accurately enough for the listener to be able to understand without too much effort. The teacher should try to keep a balance between a learner's fluency and accuracy (see chapter 1, pages 12 and 13).

Speaking in the classroom

In the classroom we need to get our learners to practise both production and interaction. Sometimes we want to get our learners to practise producing error-free language; at other times we want our learners to concentrate more on interaction and on becoming more fluent.

PORTFOLIO WORK

Look at the textbooks you use and see which of the following types of activity you can find. Which of them is the most/least controlled? Which are focused on fluency or accuracy?

– drills   – pair work   – group activities   – class activities.

Speaking activities that concentrate on getting learners to produce sounds, phrases, or grammatical structures range from activities which are controlled by the teacher to activities where the learners have more freedom to choose the language they use. Controlled activities generally focus on the learners producing language accurately, while less controlled activities focus on developing the learners' fluency.

Drills

Using drills, the teacher has a lot of control over what the learners say – they must respond to the teacher or each other, and the answers to the drill are fixed – the learners must answer correctly and according to a precise pattern. Here are three types of drill:

Substitution drills

In the drill below, the teacher practises a particular vocabulary area (or lexical set), for example, places in a town, by getting the learners to change the place – post office, supermarket, swimming pool – each time. This kind of drill is known as a substitution drill because the learners have to substitute one word for another. You can use substitution drills to practise structures as well as vocabulary.

TEACHER   Where's Mary going? [holding up a picture of a post office] She's going to the post office. Everyone, repeat. She's going to the post office.

LEARNERS   She's going to the post office.
TEACHER   Martina, where's Mary going? [holding up a picture of a supermarket]
MARTINA   She's going to the supermarket.

Transformation drills

In the transformation drill below the teacher is practising the word order of questions in the present simple by getting the learners to transform (convert or change) an affirmative sentence into a question.

TEACHER   John likes beer.
LEARNER   Does John like beer?
TEACHER   Martin plays the piano.
LEARNER   Does Martin play the piano?

Functional–situational drills

In the next drill the teacher is practising the language of a function – giving advice, for example, 'You should …'. This is known as a functional-situational drill because the learner is given different situations to respond to.

TEACHER	I've got a headache.
LEARNER	You should take an aspirin.
TEACHER	It's raining.
LEARNER	You should take an umbrella.

One problem with drills is that the learners can produce correct sentences without actually understanding what they say. We can add a meaning element to drills by varying the **prompt**, for example:

TEACHER	Pen
LEARNER	There is a pen on the table.
TEACHER	Book.
LEARNER	There is a book on the table.
TEACHER	Floor …

Another problem with drills is that they are limited in terms of keeping learners motivated – drills are by their nature repetitive. We can make drills more interesting by using simple stories. The story can be constructed in such a way that the learners are encouraged to use particular structures or functions in their responses, for example, expressing regret. The pictures below show a number of disasters which happened to a character called Albert when he took his girlfriend out for dinner.

Using the pictures you can create a drill to practise one way of expressing regret, for example:

Picture 1 He wished he hadn't been late.
Picture 2 He wished he hadn't dropped his flowers.

PORTFOLIO WORK

Think of a structure or a function which your learners need to learn or practise. Can you invent a story or situation to practise that structure using pictures and drills? Write a plan for the story and the structure or vocabulary you want to practise and try it out in your class.

As well as getting practice in producing sounds and phrases accurately, learners need to be able to interact with each other. In interactive activities the emphasis is often more on fluency and less on accuracy.

Pair work and group work

It is a good idea to put learners into groups or pairs so that they can get more speaking practice – if learners only speak to the teacher, their opportunities for practice are limited. If it takes a long time to get your learners into groups in every lesson, you can divide the learners up into set groups at the beginning of the year. This means that learners always use the same groups and do not have to spend time deciding whom to form a group with. You can change these groupings every few months if you want learners to practise working with different people. The following step-by-step approach can be a helpful way to lead into pair or group work:

1 The teacher asks questions and nominates individual learners to answer. For example, if you are practising the vocabulary for families, you can ask a learner how many brothers or sisters they have.
2 Introduce open pair work (learners speak to someone across the class). The teacher nominates learners to ask each other. For example, 'Tomas, ask Zara'.
3 Learners choose who they want to answer. Use a soft ball or a floppy toy. The learner holds this as he asks a question and then throws it to the person he would like to answer. The rules are that you can't throw it to someone who has already had it. This activity keeps the class attentive, as they don't know when it will be their turn, and it also develops social skills because they have to pay attention and include learners who haven't had a turn.
4 Do in **closed pairs** (learners speak to the person next to them) what has just been demonstrated in open pairs.

It is important that the teacher **monitors** the activity carefully and gives specific feedback on anything the learners have done well or any errors that need to be pointed out and corrected.

Types of interactive activities

Information gap activities

We often interact with other people to give or ask for information. If one learner knows or can see something that the other doesn't, this gives them a genuine reason to speak. Classroom activities that simulate this type of situation are called information gap activities. Here are some examples:

– describe and draw – one learner has a picture and has to describe it to a partner, who draws the picture.
– describe and arrange – learners have to arrange objects according to instructions from a partner.

– describe and identify – learners have to identify which picture from a series of pictures is being described by their partner.
– find the differences – in pairs each learner has a similar picture but with some differences. They have to describe their pictures to each other in order to find the differences.

Student A		
	Departs	Arrives
Oxford → Heathrow Airport (bus)	08:30	10:15
London Heathrow → Tokyo Narita	13:00	06:30 (next day)
Student B		
	Departs	Arrives
Oxford → Heathrow Airport (bus)	_____	_____
London Heathrow → Tokyo Narita	_____	_____

– asking for information – for example, about times of trains, planes, buses. One learner has the information; the other needs to go from X to Y and asks their partner for the necessary information.
– asking for and giving directions. One learner has certain places marked on a map, the other learner has different places marked.

Discussion activities

We also speak to give our opinions or to hear other people's opinions. Discussion activities give learners the chance to speak more freely and express themselves. It is helpful to structure a discussion activity by giving learners enough information about what they will be talking about, and giving them enough time to think about what they want to say. Some examples include:

– surveys: learners carry out a survey of their class (or others) on a topic of their choice, for example, how many people have pets and what kind they are. Surveys can also ask for opinions rather than facts, for example, 'What do you think about keeping pets?'. Learners can then talk about the results of the surveys in class.
– ranking activities: putting a list of items in order from the most important to the least important. For example, what qualities (you can give a list of suggestions) are most important in a teacher? What ten items from a list of twenty would you take to a desert island?
– planning: for example, learners can be given advertisements with information about plays, films, or tourist attractions in a particular place. They can then be asked to decide on a programme for a day out. They can be asked to plan other events if they are given the appropriate information. For example, they choose a restaurant or a holiday from a selection; they can plan a birthday party or other celebration.
– discussing and solving problems: the functional-situational drill for giving advice ('you should …') can be made into a more interactive activity which practises fluency by giving the learners longer problems to discuss and give advice on. For example, you can give learners invented letters from problem pages, or get them to talk about particular difficulties they have in learning English. Learners can also be given more practical problems to solve, such as preparing for an exam.

– debates: learners can be given a (controversial) statement and they have to decide whether they agree or disagree and why. This can lead to a relatively unstructured discussion of a subject, either with the whole class or in groups.

Role plays

These can be like mini-dramas. Each learner is given a character and a card with some information on it which can include information about their role and the situation. With other learners or in a group they then have to act out a situation as if they were the people on their card. Here is an example:

CUSTOMER	You bought a shirt yesterday. When you got home you noticed that there was a mark on the sleeve. You take it back to the shop. You do not want to buy another shirt; you want your money back.
MANAGER	You are the manager of the shop. Your policy is that you can only exchange clothes; you cannot give customers their money back. You always try to be polite to customers, but you cannot change store policy without writing to head office.
SHOP ASSISTANT	You work in a shop. Yesterday a customer bought a shirt. You noticed that it had a mark on the sleeve so you told her/him and gave her/him a discount.

Games

Games are often useful to liven up a lesson. Some examples of games giving speaking practice include:

– I spy: the teacher chooses something from the classroom, for example, the blackboard, and says to the learners, 'I spy with my little eye something beginning with *b*', giving them only the first letter. The learners have to guess what it is. Learners can also play this game in groups.
– Twenty questions: the teacher thinks of a famous person. The learners have to ask yes/no questions to find out who the famous person is, for example, 'Is he a man?' – 'Yes', 'Can he sing?' – 'No'. Learners can also play this game in groups.

Informal interaction

The teacher and class can interact informally, asking each other what they are going to do at the weekend, talking about recent news stories, telling jokes or personal stories. The teacher can ask the learners to prepare a joke or story to tell the rest of the class.

Feedback and correction

Learners need encouragement and they need to know when they are making mistakes that might cause other people not to understand or misunderstand them. Teachers should also use the opportunity to praise learners for getting something right, doing something well, trying hard, and showing a positive attitude towards learning. This could be when they produce an accurate sentence, do an amusing role play, make an interesting contribution to a discussion, or show that they can use a new item of vocabulary.

It is more difficult to decide when to correct. Teachers can choose to correct as soon as the mistake is made or at the end of the activity or class. The advantage of immediate correction is that the learner can correct the error and use the corrected language for the rest of the activity. The disadvantage is that it can break the flow of communication and possibly demotivate or embarrass the learner.

ACTIVITY 5

What do you think the advantages and disadvantages of correcting at the end of an activity or lesson might be?

Summary

Speaking is a complex process which involves constructing a message in a form that other people can understand, and delivering the message using the correct pronunciation, stress, and intonation. Speaking also involves interaction – communicating with other people. To do this learners need to be able to respond to what other people say, and use the language appropriate for the situation they are in and the person they are talking to. At the same time they need to be accurate and fluent enough for the other person to understand and to fit into the flow of conversation. To be able to do all of this learners need lots and lots of practice, encouragement, and correction.

Case study

Go to the 'Case study' section at the back of the book and listen to a teacher talk about their experiences of teaching speaking.

6 READING

In this chapter we explore:

– the reading process
– reading skills
– reading in the classroom
– reading for younger learners.

The reading process

Here are some of the things we read:

– novels	– menus
– text messages	– coursebooks
– letters	– street signs
– emails	– labels
– timetables	– application forms
– newspapers	– websites
– magazines	– flight or train information boards.

We call these different types of reading material 'texts'.

ACTIVITY 1

Can you add any more items to the list of texts above?

There are two basic types of texts – authentic and non-authentic. Examples of authentic texts are newspaper articles, website pages, emails, packaging and labels, and so on. Non-authentic texts are written especially for learners using imaginary contexts and simplified vocabulary and sentence construction, for example, a reading text in an elementary coursebook, a **reader** for young learners.

There are differences between the texts in terms of the way they are organized. For example, an email is laid out in a different way from a letter, a website looks very different from a textbook. The writing style or **register** changes according to the text. For example, the style of an email from a friend is very different from a chapter in a history book. Texts vary in length

– from street signs, text messages, emails, newspaper articles, short stories, to novels. The way we read will depend partly on how long the text is.

We read for a variety of reasons. We might read for information – to find out how to do something, for example, an instruction manual for a computer; or to learn about something, for example, a history or science textbook. We might need to know what time a lesson starts or when a train arrives. We might read something as part of communicating with someone, for example, an email or a text message. We might read for pleasure, for example, a novel, magazine article, or website. We might read something for our studies or our job. It might be a combination of some or all these factors.

Reading is also an important way for learners to access new language and practise language they have already met.

Reading skills

Learners need to develop the following skills:

– learning to read in various ways, for example, skimming and scanning
– adapting the way they read according to the text and their reason for reading
– reading 'actively' – using a dictionary, guessing or asking about unknown words
– understanding the relationship between sentences – see chapter 7, page 88
– helping understanding by using textual and visual clues, i.e. headings, the way the text is organized into paragraphs, punctuation, signal words, pictures, typography, and so on.
– using contextual clues – where the learners are, what they and other people are doing at the time
– inferring meaning
– guessing meaning – see page 2
– background knowledge of the culture about which they are reading.

Learners need to be able to interpret a text in order to be able to understand the message being communicated. To do this they need to know how sentences and text are put together. For example:

ASBO for homeless man

An anti-social behaviour order has been given to a 42-year-old man after complaints were received about him over a four-year period.

John Simms, of no fixed address, was convicted at Reading Crown Court of one offence of possessing an offensive weapon and two charges of harassment.

It follows complaints that he acted in an anti-social manner where he used to live in Windmill Road, Whitchurch.

He was given a seven-month jail term, but freed due to the time spent in custody.

To understand this text we need to understand:

– the meaning of 'ASBO' and other words related to social behaviour
– how the subject is referred to in different ways through the text – 'homeless man', '42-year-old man', 'John Simms', 'he'
– something about contemporary English society
– general rules about how phrases, clauses, and sentences are formed. (See chapter 3 for more details about how the language works.)

When we read the eye usually moves from top to bottom and left to right across the page or screen. Our brain holds short sections of the text long enough in its **working memory** to decode it and relate it to the previous part and anticipate the next part of the text. The reader also uses their knowledge of the world and language in their **long-term memory** to help them understand the text.

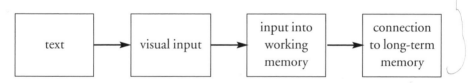

Our brain anticipates what is coming next by using clues from the text (the words, the way it is organized and laid out), what we know about similar texts, and the context (the situation).

ACTIVITY 2

What do you think comes next in this text?

The waiter came up to his table. 'Anything to drink?' he asked.
'Yeah. Great,' said Nick, '............'

Skimming and scanning

The ability to read something quickly and efficiently is an important skill for learners to acquire. Skimming and scanning are two ways of doing this.

Reading for gist / skimming

When we read for gist or 'skim' a text we do not try to understand everything in it – we read through it fairly quickly to get a general idea of what it is about. For example, when you first pick up a textbook, you look through it quickly to see if it suits your class – is it the right level? are the topics interesting? does it cover the right language areas? and so on. When you look at a newspaper you skim the headlines to see which articles are of interest. In a bookshop you look at the blurb on the back cover of a book to see if it is worth reading. We also skim longer texts when we do not have the time to read every word or line.

Scanning

This is the kind of reading you do when you want to find out about something specific, for example, get a particular piece of information from a text. We run our eyes over the text looking for a specific word or phrase. We scan a text, for example, when we are looking up a word in a dictionary, or reading the TV page to find out what time a particular television programme is on. We also scan when we are looking something up in a telephone directory, or in an index to find references to specific topics, for example.

Reading for detail

Skimming and scanning are done fairly rapidly, but if we want to follow a text in detail we read more slowly. So, for example, if we are reading an instruction manual which tells us how to assemble a piece of furniture, we need to follow each stage of the text carefully. If we are reading a book in order to get information for our studies, we will also tend to read more carefully and may make notes as we read.

Reading for pleasure

If we are reading a novel, a magazine, or a letter from a friend we are reading for enjoyment or to relax. We will often read some parts of the text carefully and others more quickly depending on our personal interests.

Reading for general meaning

We often read at a steady pace, occasionally skipping parts, rereading some parts, taking note of some details, and ignoring others.

ACTIVITY 3

Look at the website on page 73. To find out the following information do you need to skim, scan, or both?

1 How many Oxford Bookworms stories are there?
2 Can you buy books online?
3 Where do you go if you want to find new resources?

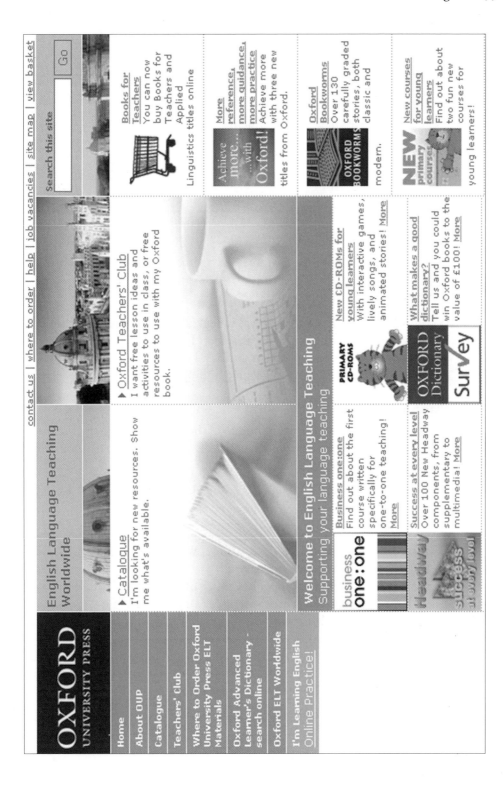

Inferring meaning

Sometimes part of the meaning of a text is not explicitly stated – we have to infer it, i.e. use reasoning and the text to make our own conclusions. For example, what can we infer from the following?

> There were five guests. Four of them were really charming.

> He waited for her outside school every day, but she was always with her girlfriends. Then one day he saw her with Bob, his best friend.

Reading in the classroom

Reading activities aim to:

– introduce and develop reading skills which are useful outside the classroom
– introduce or practise language.

Learners should read as widely and as independently in English as they can. Extensive reading of material such as readers is an excellent way of developing reading skills and increasing vocabulary. Learners should be encouraged to choose what they read and given help finding reading material.

Planning a lesson

First of all you must decide what the aim of the lesson is. To do this you need to consider your learners' needs – which skills do they need to develop? How can you help them develop these skills?

Choosing the right text for your class is one of the most important decisions you have to make. Consider the following:

– topic: What are your class interested in – world affairs, sport, films, travel? What do they know about the topic? Will you need to give some background information first?
– level: What level are your class? How much of the vocabulary in the text do they know? How complex are the sentences and text overall?
– length: How long is the text? How long will it take to read? Reading takes time and is seen by some learners as a waste of classroom time. So you need to keep material to be read in the classroom reasonably short and make the activities as communicative as possible. One alternative is to tell the learners to read a text before coming to class.

We can break a reading lesson down into three stages:

– pre-reading stage: activities that prepare the learners for what they will read and set the task for the second stage

– reading stage: activities that provide a purpose for reading and enable the
  teacher to monitor the learners
– post-reading stage: activities for checking, giving feedback, and follow-up
  work.

Pre-reading activities

Pre-reading activities are designed to:

– set a task for the learners
– help the learners prepare for the task
– motivate the learners to read.

Tasks can be divided into two basic types:

– answering questions
– 'doing' something, for example, drawing, moving, problem solving.

Answering questions

Teachers use questions to check whether the learners have understood a text.
For example, if the learners have read a short story – who is who? what
happened? did it turn out all right in the end? For an email – did the learners
understand the message? i.e. what did the writer want to know? what should
the reader do next? and so on. The questions should reflect the type of
reading skill being practised, i.e.

– gist questions
– detailed comprehension questions
– scanning questions.

Questions can also ask the reader to interact with the text – comment on it,
evaluate it, say what they liked about it or found interesting.

Questions can also be set to be answered in the pre-reading activity and then
checked in the reading activity, for example, prediction activities using a
news headline:

    Lead singer quits band.

The learners could predict why the singer left, what the singer will do next,
what will happen to the band, and so on. The teacher can give them question
word prompts to help:

Who	Where
What	Why
When	How (much, far, big, etc.)

Questions can also focus on the language. For example, 'Which words in the
text refer to food?' How is 'like' used in the text? See page 106 for more details
about questions.

'Doing' something
A task will encourage the learners to interact directly with the text. For example:

– jigsaw reading, for example, reading about two famous people – how are they similar? how are they different?
– problem solving, for example, who was the murderer?
– moving, for example, miming a story
– order, for example, in time sequence; prioritize according to likes/preferences, etc.

Pre-reading activities should help the learners achieve the aims of the activity, i.e.

– stimulate what they already know about the topic
– provide them with background information that they need before they read
– help them with words and phrases they will need to know.

You can get learners to **brainstorm**, that is, try to think of as many ideas as possible associated with the topic. They may use a mind map like the one below to write down their ideas.

ACTIVITY 4

Look at this mind map and think of some words to go under the headings.

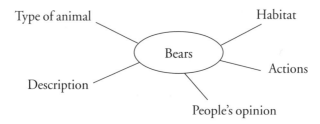

Figure 6.1   'Bear' mind map

You can give some key words and ask your learners to note down what they know about the topic. You can get the learners to do this in groups. If you brainstorm in the learners' L1 to start with, you can then translate the key words into English and write them in a mind map.

Pre-teaching vocabulary
Remember that at this stage it is important to teach only the new words which are necessary to understand the text. It is useful to distinguish between receptive and productive vocabulary:

– receptive vocabulary includes the words which are necessary to understand the text, but in general are not useful for your learners at their present level
– productive vocabulary includes the words which appear in the text which are useful and therefore should be focused on fully so that the learners can use them correctly.

For example, you may wish your learners to read a text called 'A Day in the Life of a Farmer'. There may be some vegetables mentioned in the text, for example, 'celeriac', or 'marrow', which may distract them because they do not know them, but which you decide are not useful for them to be able to use themselves at this stage. It is probably enough to give them a simple explanation that they are types of vegetable. It is not necessary to check they understand exactly what each vegetable is or to practise the pronunciation and spelling of these words. In general it may be sufficient to give simple definitions or translations for vocabulary which is pre-taught for receptive purposes only.

However, there may be other words in the text which form a coherent and useful group (we looked at this idea of a lexical set in chapter 3, p.33) which you decide to teach your learners for their productive use. For example, you may want to use a recipe text with your learners, so you decide to teach a range of words associated with cooking, for example, 'fry', 'roast', 'grill', and 'bake'. It is often possible to integrate the pre-teaching vocabulary stage of the lesson with the stage where you are creating interest and stimulating learners' background knowledge. Here are two examples:

Example 1
Your learners are going to do reading activities related to a TV guide. First ask your learners to tell you what programmes they like watching on TV and then ask them to rank the following list in order according to which is their favourite. You can supply definitions or examples for any that they don't know, or they can use their dictionaries to look the words up.

Cartoons	History programmes
Documentaries	Children's magazine programmes
Pop music programmes	Comedy programmes
News	Drama
Films	

Example 2
You are going to read about a visit to relatives. The following words all appear in a story in this order. Read the words and discuss with your partner any that you are not sure about. What do you think the story is about?

aunt	dinner	shouting
table	evening	cat
fish	steal	door
cousins	chase	vegetables

Reading activities

Here are three types of reading activities:

– teacher–learner interaction activities
– learner–learner interaction activities
– text-only activities: the learners read the text all the way through, answering questions or doing the activities set.

Teacher–learner interaction activities

You can stop learners during their reading to ask them questions. For example, questions about what they have just read, or prediction questions about what they expect to read next. This activity works well with short stories where the learners will be more involved if you are asking questions about the text as they are reading. These questions can be written after certain paragraphs in the text if you are making a worksheet.

Learner–learner interaction activities

These involve the learners interacting with one another and the text, for example:

– jigsaw reading: each learner has one half of a text. They have to ask questions to find out what is in the other learner's text.
– problem solving: a group of five learners have five different texts, for example about a murder. They have to share the information to find out who the murderer was.
– reading race: put the class into small teams and give each team a copy of the text. The players take it in turns to come out to the front and collect a question on a slip of paper, a different team member writes the number of the question and the answer, and then shows it to the teacher, who then gives them a different question. They continue like this until all the questions are answered and the first team to finish are the winners. This activity is a good way of encouraging learners to scan read.

Text-only activities

– ordering: the learners have to put a list of events into the right time sequence, for example, a recipe.
– jumbled paragraphs: a story is cut up and learners have to put the paragraphs into the correct order.
– note-taking: if it is a factual text, learners can take notes of the main points as they read. The note-taking can be structured for them by giving them appropriate headings under which to write their notes.
– checking pre-reading activities: if you have done prediction, question-forming, brainstorming, ranking or discussion activities in the pre-reading stage, it is obviously appropriate to use these as the basis for the reading activities. For example: Were your predictions correct? What are the answers to the questions you made? Is there any other information in the

text that you did not come up with in your brainstorming? For example, if you are getting the learners to answer the questions they wrote down about the pop star headline, you can tell them that they have one minute to read the article and find as many answers as they can to their questions – setting a time limit helps learners to understand that they must read fast and not worry about understanding every word. Ask them to note those answers down.

– identifying a picture related to the text: for example, learners read a letter in which a girl tells her friend about her new hairstyle. They read the letter and tick the correct picture.

– following directions: for example, learners read a note giving them directions to a friend's new house. They look at a map and draw a line from where they are to their friend's new house.

– drawing a picture from a text: for example, learners are given a police description of a criminal who is wanted in connection with a burglary. They read the description and draw a 'Wanted' poster.

– choosing a title or headline: for example, learners read a newspaper article and decide on a suitable headline.

ACTIVITY 5

Look at the text below and at the comprehension questions that follow. Decide what each of the questions is asking the learners to do:

My mother started going out to work when I was six years old. As far as I remember, apart from going to the office, she never went out and no friends came to the house. She worked very hard, but she seemed cheerful and **we** enjoyed ourselves as much as we could without my dad, who had died just before by sixth birthday. When I was 12 my mother went to work in London for six months and I moved from the flat in Rome, which we had shared with my dad, to Ancona, to my grandmother's house. I was sad to go because I left all my friends **there** but my grandmother was kind to me and spent a lot of time with me. We used to telephone my mother on Sunday evenings and after **that** my grandmother would play a game with me, because I often felt sad.

Questions

1 This text is taken from:

   − a newspaper article
   − a letter
   − an autobiography.

2 Put the following events in chronological order:

   a He telephoned his mother on Sunday evenings.
   b He went to Ancona.
   c He lived with his grandmother.
   d His father died.
   e His mother started working.
   f He lived in Rome.
   g His mother went to work in London.

3 What two things show that his grandmother was kind to him?

4 How do we know he missed his father?

5 What do the words in bold refer to?

6 'Cheerful' (line 3) means:

   a happy
   b tired
   c unhappy

Post-reading activities

As with listening, this stage can involve other skills, such as writing, speaking, or vocabulary development.

Vocabulary

You can use some of the words in the text as a springboard for language focus/vocabulary learning activities after the reading text has been used for reading comprehension and reading skills development. For example, you may use a text about a holiday, which has the words 'train' and 'travel'. You could then use this as the basis for a lexical set of words in a language focus follow-up: 'car', 'plane', 'journey', 'arrive', 'suitcase', 'hotel'. Learners could then write a paragraph describing how they get to school or to work.

You can highlight words that may be new to learners and get them to work out what they mean from the context. For example, you can do this by giving them multiple-choice options for the meanings of the words. These activities build learners' confidence so that they realize that they do not have to look up every unknown word in their dictionary.

Learners can write down the meanings of some of the new words they have guessed during reading, and can check these with the teacher (and each other) afterwards.

Writing
Ask learners to change the ending of the text, or rewrite the last few sentences if it is a story. Most texts can be used as a model for a writing activity. If you analyse the organization of a text, for example, in an argumentative text, this might mean identifying how the arguments for and against an idea are organized, and can provide a useful model for learners' own writing. Learners can also give the text a different title.

Speaking
One person starts and each person following adds a bit more of the story. Learners can also act out the story in a role play or draw a flowchart of the plot. In the example of the pop star mentioned on page 75, you can get the learners to tell you what they now know about the star from the notes they have made.

Grammar
You can develop exercises which encourage learners to notice or to practise particular language structures. See Figure 6.2.

Creating a reading environment
Here are two ways in which you can focus on reading English which learners might already know, and which they see in the environment around them in advertisements, shop signs, magazines, and so on. Obviously this will only work for learners who can read in their own language, but even younger children can be asked to look for English words in the world around them.

– Try to collect real examples of English words in print. For example, food and other products that are made in your country but exported to English-speaking countries usually have labels (and other information) in English, as well as other languages. English words can also appear in children's magazines or comics or on computer games.

Hannah Lean is 17, and already has a place to study Psychology at university in October. However, she has a choice. She could:

- go to university this October.
- get a job near her home for a year, then go to university next October.
- work abroad for a year and then go to university next October.

At the moment, the second possibility sounds attractive. ¹ If she gets a job and lives at home, she'll be able to save money. ² That will help her when she goes to university. On the other hand, ³ she probably won't get another chance to live abroad unless she does it now. Hannah says, 'It's a difficult choice. ⁴ If I have to make big decisions, I always talk to mum and dad first. But in the end, I do what I want!'

1 Read 'Hannah's choice', then answer these questions about sentences 1 to 4.

a In sentence 1, what tenses are used? Is she sure that she'll get a job?

b In sentence 2, what tenses are used? Is she sure she'll go to university?

c In sentence 3, what tenses are used? Does *unless* mean *if* or *if + not*?

d In sentence 4, there are two present simple verbs. Why?

e In sentences 1 and 4, can you replace *if* with *when*, and keep the same meaning? Why / why not?

Figure 6.2 Noticing grammar in a reading text (from Natural English Intermediate*)*

– Advertisements that have English words in them can be a useful source. For younger learners you can find examples of advertisements for children's toys or other children's products. You could even take photographs of English signs and advertisements that you see. Bring these into the classroom and ask your learners to look out for examples as well.

Using real examples is important because these short texts will convey a message. They will help learners to understand that reading involves understanding a message, rather than just sounding out the letters of a word.

In order to motivate learners to read it is important to create a positive reading environment. This is particularly true for younger learners but some of the following ideas also apply to older learners.

– Label things in the classroom, for example, 'paper', 'pencils', 'door', 'desk', 'board'.
– Display learners' work – this will encourage them to read each other's work and to present their own work neatly.
– Many ELT publishers produce very useful posters for the classroom.
– Make your own posters of classroom language, for example, 'Can I borrow your pen/rubber/ruler?'
– Write instructions on the board.
– Have 'I heard /read this' posters on which children write English words and phrases they come across.
– Present reading in a variety of forms, for example, embedded in board games, crosswords, codes, etc.
– Create a reading corner. This is a comfortable space in the school or classroom with a selection of books where learners can go to read.

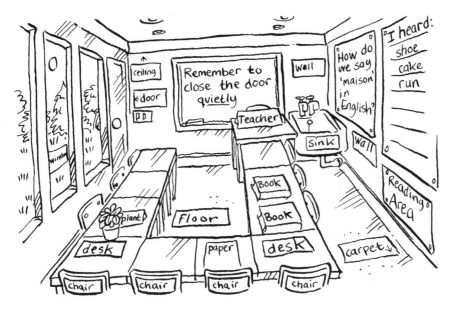

Reading for younger learners

An excellent way to motivate younger learners to read is to read to them. Not only do stories expose them to the patterns of English but they can also create a positive attitude to books and the printed word. Here are some points to consider:

– look for a good story with pictures that illustrate the meaning. Make sure that it's not too long and that there are opportunities for the children to get involved. With younger children stories with repetition work well.
– if you don't have many reading books, you can create your own
– discuss the cover, the title, and the author
– use your voice: slow down, pause, and **elicit**
– be prepared: it helps if you know the story well before you begin
– eye contact: try to read from one side, with the book facing the children. This allows you to maintain eye contact with the children which is essential for control and for conveying the drama of the story.
– use the pictures to pre-teach key vocabulary
– with younger children you can point to the words as you read, this will encourage them to start decoding letters and words
– encourage the children to predict what will happen
– find out what they know about the topic
– encourage them to join in with any repetition, sound effects, mime, and so on.

Interactive reading for younger learners

Teachers of English to younger learners are primarily concerned with getting children listening and speaking. However, we can introduce reading in a manageable, fun way, providing we structure carefully the way we present the reading activities. Here are some ideas for active participation:

– get the children to draw, for example, a clown – 'Look at the clown. He's wearing a hat, a scarf and a long coat ...'
– get the children to match, for example, pictures of pets to children – 'Sandra's got a dog', and so on.
– get the children to colour things in, for example, 'The clown's hat is red, and his scarf blue', and so on.

All these activities give younger learners a reason to read and the amount of text is limited. Once the children become confident with reading at sentence level they can progress to short texts.

Summary

In this chapter we have looked at the reading process and at different ways of reading. We have looked at the kind of activities we can use to practise reading in class and at how to structure a reading lesson. We have looked at reading with younger learners, and at ways of creating a reading environment in class.

Case study

Go to the 'Case study' section at the back of the book and listen to a teacher talk about their experiences of teaching reading.

7 WRITING

In this chapter we explore:

– the writing process
– writing skills
– writing in the classroom.

The writing process

We saw in chapter 5 that speaking involves putting together a combination of sounds in a particular order to form words, phrases, and sentences. When we are writing we have to do something similar except that we do it with letters rather than sounds. We put these together to form words, phrases, clauses, and sentences, and put sentences together to make a coherent text. We write a variety of things, for example:

– letters	– emails	– diaries	– application forms
– lists (shopping, 'To do', etc.)	– memos	– notes	– postcards.

ACTIVITY 1

Can you add any more text types to the list above?

We write for many different reasons – to pass on information and opinions, to ask questions, request or offer something, to entertain, to keep a record, to organize our thoughts, as part of the assessment process, and so on. Sometimes we write to communicate and this can be quite interactive and relatively immediate, for example, when we are texting or emailing someone. These texts are often quite short and simple. We might write longer texts as part of our studies, for a composition, a short story, or an examination. For work we may be required to write reports or formal letters, or fill in application forms.

When we write we should think about the reader/s. Who are they? What is our relationship with them? Why are they going to read what we write? We then need to adjust the content and style accordingly by using formal or informal language and the appropriate layout and conventions. We can break down the writing process into three stages:

- preparation – think about the reader; consider why we are writing; think about the content; decide the appropriate layout and style
- draft – put our ideas together in a draft form. This is probably all we need for things like shopping lists and memos, but for longer texts we need to do more work.
- editing and rewriting – we will probably need to rewrite several times so that the text is coherent, clear, and has few or no mistakes.

Figure 7.1 shows how we might produce a longer text such as a composition.

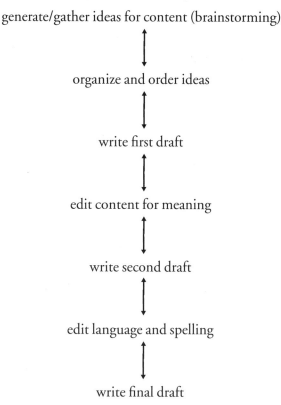

generate/gather ideas for content (brainstorming)

organize and order ideas

write first draft

edit content for meaning

write second draft

edit language and spelling

write final draft

Figure 7.1 The writing process

Notice that the arrows between the stages in the diagram of the writing process go in both directions. This is because the process of writing and re-writing does not just develop in a straight line. For example, you might decide at the first draft stage to re-order some of the ideas, or to take some ideas out and put different ones in. So when we write we move backwards and forwards between the different stages.

Writing is also part of the language learning process. We write:

– to practise the language
– to reinforce the language we have learnt
– to help memorization
– as a way of recording language
– as part of being assessed.

Writing skills

Learners need to develop the following skills:

– handwriting: forming letters, connected script, upper and lower case, starting from top left and writing across the page
– spelling
– use of punctuation
– forming sentences: word order, endings, relationships. (See chapter 3.)
– writing longer texts: **coherence** and **cohesion**
– using the appropriate layout
– using the appropriate level of formality
– study skills: making notes, keeping records, etc.

Handwriting

Learners may need to work on their handwriting skills if:

– their L1 is not based on the Roman script, for example, Japanese, Chinese, Korean, Arabic.
– they are not used to writing with a pen, for example, they are more used to using a keyboard
– they haven't had the opportunity to develop their writing skills in their L1
– they are young learners.

Spelling

Spelling causes problems for lots of learners because there is no one-to-one relationship between sounds and spelling in English, for example, 'i' may be pronounced /aɪ/, /ɜː/, or /ɪ/, and /aɪ/ may be spelt with an 'i' or a 'y'. (See chapter 3 for more details.)

Punctuation

Learners need to know the basic elements of punctuation:

– capital letters: for the beginning of a sentence, place names, and so on
– full stops: for the end of a sentence
– commas: to mark the ends of phrases and clauses
– question marks: to signal a question
– apostrophe: to show an abbreviation or possessive.

Forming sentences

English sentence formation is complicated and there are many possible patterns. Here is an example from a newspaper article:

> More than one million *people* have begun to *evacuate* the Gulf *Coast* of the United States ahead of Hurricane Rita.

This first sentence has a basic 'subject – verb – object' pattern, i.e. 'People evacuate coast'. The writer gives us more information about the time by adding a prepositional phrase at the end of the sentence, 'ahead of Hurricane Rita'.

ACTIVITY 2

Look at the three main parts of the basic sentence, 'People evacuate coast'. In what other ways does the writer add to this basic sentence?

Forming connected text

Here is the rest of the text about Hurricane Rita:

> The storm, which has been upgraded to Category Five, is heading towards Texas with winds of 175 mph. Experts say the hurricane could be the most intense ever to hit Texas, and one of the most powerful seen on the US mainland. President George Bush has declared a state of emergency in Texas and neighbouring Louisiana. He asked people to pay attention to evacuation orders. New Orleans is not in the likely path of the storm. However, engineers are racing to repair the city's flood defence system, in case rain from Rita causes yet more floods.

We need to consider two questions:

– Is the text cohesive – do the parts fit together?
– Is it coherent – does it make sense?

The parts fit together in a variety of ways. For example, the way in which the event is referred to: 'Hurricane Rita', 'the storm', 'the hurricane'. In English the same subject is often referred to using different words or phrases. Pronouns are used in the same way, for example, 'President George Bush' and 'He'. The verb 'evacuate' in the first sentence links up with 'evacuation orders' in the final sentence. 'However' links two sentences and indicates that the information in the first sentence is in contrast with the second. We are given extra information about the storm in the relative clause 'which has been upgraded to Category Five'.

The text is organized in a way that gives us the main point first, i.e. that people are evacuating the Gulf coast, then it gives us the supporting information about why, i.e. details about the storm and the declaration from President Bush.

We can now look in more detail at the features of a written text.

Avoiding repetition

We generally try to avoid repeating the same word by using an alternative word or phrase, as we saw above, using words like 'there', 'one' or 'now'; by using pronouns (him, he, it); or by missing out the word altogether. For example, instead of:

> **Angela** went to buy a newspaper. **Angela** took **a newspaper** from the shelf. **Angela** gave **the newspaper** to the shopkeeper.

We might write:

> **Angela** went to buy a newspaper. **She** took **one** from the shelf and gave **it** to the shopkeeper.

Linking

Normally a text flows more easily if some of the sentences are connected with linking devices such as 'and', 'because', or 'but'. In the above example we combined two sentences using 'and':

> She took one from the shelf **and** gave it to the shopkeeper.

ACTIVITY 3

Which words would you change in the following text to avoid repetition?

John is a journalist. John went to London to meet Angela. Angela is John's girlfriend. John met Angela at the station. John and Angela went to a restaurant and had lunch.

Relative clauses

We can put information together and avoid repetition by putting additional information into a separate clause, for example:

> John, who is a journalist, went to London to meet his girlfriend, Angela.

Or we can simply link the two sets of information together. Here are examples using 'who', 'where', and 'which':

> I saw the woman. The woman had dark hair.
> I saw the woman **who** had dark hair.

> He went to a restaurant. He met his wife there
> He went to a restaurant **where** he met his wife.

He has a dog. It has a red collar.
He has a dog **which** has a red collar.

ACTIVITY 4

Make a cohesive text from the sentences below by joining them together using the words in brackets and removing any unnecessary repetition.

Dorna lived in London. Dorna went to school in London. (*where*)

Dorna liked her school. Dorna's parents moved to Manchester. Dorna's mother found a new job in Manchester. (*but, where*)

Dorna went to a new school. Dorna made lots of new friends. (*and*)

Dorna found a boyfriend. The boyfriend went to the same school. (*then, who*)

Dorna got very good grades in her exams. Her boyfriend failed all his exams. (*but*)

Dorna decided not to go to university. She wanted to stay with her boyfriend. (*because*)

Signalling
The writer should 'signal' to the reader what is happening in the text. For example:

– 'First of all' – this signals the beginning of a sequence
– 'Next' – this signals that we are moving from one part of a sequence to the next
– 'However' – this indicates that we are contrasting one statement with another.

Using appropriate layout

The layouts of a letter, email, and memo are very different. Learners need to be aware of the various elements that make up these types of texts. See Figure 7.2.

Using the appropriate level of formality

Levels of formality depend on people's relationship to each other – whether they are friends or don't know each other, whether someone is senior or junior, and so on. For example, the first text below would be written by one friend to another, the second would be a formal invitation from an organization:

Hi Jo,

Fancy getting together for a drink after work?

Bob

ELLIS AUTOPARTS INC.

1021 East 160th Street Bronx, NY 10443
phone: 718-561-2000
email: ellis@autoparts.com www.ellisautoparts.com

Victor Duma
Sales Department
Colorado Autos Inc.
4610 Harrison Road
Denver, CO 80116

July 23, 2005

Subject: Catalog

Dear Mr. Duma,

Enclosed please find our latest catalog, which you requested during our phone conversation yesterday. You will see that it contains a number of interesting new items.

I look forward to hearing from you.

Sincerely,

Barbara Windsor

Barbara Windsor (Ms.)

Reply Forward Print Flag

From:	Kweston@wgassociates.com
Date:	
To:	dalvarez@ajc.com
Cc:	
Subject:	Conference
📎	Conference schedule.pdf

Dear David

I have attached the conference schedule as requested. You will see that your presentation is on Saturday morning. If you have any questions, please get in touch.

Best wishes,

Karen

MESA SPORTS SUPPLIES

MEMO

To:	All employees
From:	Vincent Ohly
Date:	Jan 23, 2006

Following the successful launch of the computer training department last year, we now plan to offer a range of new computer courses to all employees. Please discuss your training requirements with your manager by June 1 and enroll for a course by June 10.

vincent ohly

Vincent Ohly
Personnel Manager

Figure 7.2   A letter, an email, and a memo (from Writing for the Real World *2).*

Dear Mr. Fensome,

The Academy would be delighted if you were able to attend the formal dinner at Hawton Manor.

Yours sincerely,
Mary O'Brien

Here are some examples of the elements that make up formal or informal language:

– vocabulary   'attend' (formal); 'get together' (informal)

– forms of address 'Mr'/'Ms'/'Mrs' + surname (formal); first name (informal)

– salutations   'Dear', 'Yours sincerely' (more formal); 'Hi', 'Cheers', 'Bye' (informal)

– fixed phrases   '… would be delighted' (formal); '(Do you) fancy …?'(informal)

– full/short forms 'I would' (formal); 'I'd' (informal)

Study skills

Learners need to develop the skills of note taking and record keeping. Note taking is an essential skill in the classroom particularly if learners are going to be studying academically at some stage. During a lesson the teacher should always give learners time to make notes, make sure that whatever they themselves write on the board is clear and relevant, and monitor learners' note taking and give advice if necessary.

Learners should also be encouraged to keep a record of new language. This could be a new word, phrase, or grammatical item. For vocabulary, learners should be encouraged to note down the word, how the word is pronounced, the type of word it is, the words that it is associated with (collocations), and an example sentence, for example:

Word	Type	Pronunciation	Collocations	Sentence
book	verb	/bʊk/	a room, a holiday	I booked a room for one night.

ACTIVITY 5

How would you advise your learners to record any new grammar that they learn?

Writing in the classroom

Writing activities in the classroom are used:

– to develop writing skills
– as part of the process of language learning.

As we have seen, learners need to practise a wide range of writing skills. The first part of this section gives details of the types of activities that can be used to develop these skills.

In the next section we will look at how writing activities support the process of language learning in terms of vocabulary, functions, and grammar.

Handwriting

Some learners need to practise forming letters. To start with they need to form single, lower case letters, for example:

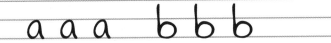

Learners need to be able to write on a straight line, keep the size of the letters regular, and form the letters accurately. When you introduce a new letter write it on the board so that the learners can see you forming the letter. Describe the form of the letter as you write. It is also useful to say the letter, i.e. /eɪ/, /bː/, and so on. Then give the learners a chance to practise. Check the results and demonstrate how to form the letter again if necessary.

Once they are able to write lower case letters they can move on to capital letters, writing their own names, friends' names, place names, and so on.

When they are ready they can move on to connected writing. It is best to start with common combinations of letters, for example 'ch' which can easily be linked together:

Spelling

As we saw in chapter 3, the relationship between spelling and sounds in English is complex, with no one-to-one relationship between them. To help learners overcome this problem it is useful to take them through the sound and spelling systems and help them to relate the two. One way of doing this is to chose two sounds that sound similar to your learners, for example, for Japanese learners /æ/ and /ʌ/ as in 'cap' and 'cup'. Dictate a short text that contains both sounds. Ask the learners to read it back to you, spelling the /æ/ or /ʌ/ each time they occur. Give the learners more practice with any words that they have difficulty with.

Punctuation

One way to practise punctuation is to provide a text stripped of all the punctuation and ask the class to rewrite it with the punctuation restored, for example:

> hi my names mika i'm finnish i live in a flat outside helsinki where do you live i have one sister called kerttu shes older than me have you got any brothers or sisters im 14 i really like running and swimming in lakes there are lots of lakes in my country where do you live what do you like doing in your free time i also love rock music do you i cant wait to hear from you

Forming sentences

There are a variety of activities to practise sentence building, for example:

– **gap fill**
– dictation
– reordering
– finishing sentences.

For examples of these see pages 125 to 127.

Writing longer texts

As we have seen, writing longer texts such as compositions, reports, short stories, letters, and so on requires a range of sub-skills and use of language, and learners need considerable practice in these. Longer writing activities are usually divided into three stages:

– pre-writing stage – the teacher sets the task; learners prepare for what they will write
– writing stage – the learners do the task, for example, writing a report, a story, a letter
– post-writing stage – feedback and follow-up work.

Pre-writing stage

In order to prepare for a writing activity the learners can:

– think about the audience or reader
– brainstorm – for example, if learners are preparing to write about global-
  ization, they should note the arguments for and against. If they are going
  to write a description, they can brainstorm some relevant vocabulary.
– gather information – for example, by doing a questionnaire or reading
  research
– practise specific writing skills, for example, using punctuation, using linking words, and so on
– practise particular language forms, for example, the past tense if they are
  going write a short story
– decide on the content – what to include and not include
– look at a model text – for example, the punctuation, use of paragraphs,
  cohesive devices, layout, etc. in an example that is similar to the one the
  learners will be writing
– write an outline or plan.

Writing stage

As we saw in Figure 7.1 learners write a draft, edit, and rewrite until they
complete the final version. They should refer back to decisions made in the
pre-writing stage regarding audience, content, aims, and outline. They
should also check for use of any language they practised and make sure that
their text is both cohesive and coherent.

The learners can work in groups and give advice and feedback to each other.
As the learners go through this process the teacher should monitor and also
give advice and feedback. At the same time teachers should let the learners
work as independently as possible.

Post-writing stage

The learners can share or display their finished work and give overall
comments on how successful their work has been. The teacher can do
follow-up work on any area of the language that still needs work.

ACTVITY 6

Look at the three writing tasks below and decide how you would plan the three
stages for each of them:

1 Writing a short story – the learners write a short story in the past using the four
  pictures in Figure 7.3.

Figure 7.3   Using a picture story (from Teaching Grammar*)*

2 Writing a report – the learners write a report on the most popular class pastimes, i.e. what people do during their spare time.

3 Writing about someone – learners use a picture on the board as the basis for a description of someone.

Here are some other ideas for writing activities:

– Learners write notes to each other, for example, asking to borrow a ruler; inviting a friend to a party; arranging to go out.
– They can write a quiz for other learners to answer, for example, about sport, general knowledge, famous people.
– They can design their own birthday cards.
– They can write instructions telling another learner how to do something, for example, how to make a paper aeroplane, how to play their favourite game, how to get to their house.
– They can write labels for things in the classroom or drawings, for example, the parts of the body or parts of a vehicle.
– They can make posters for their class.
– They can write letters to real people, for example, they can write to their local newspaper, or they can find pen friends to write to.
– They can take on longer writing tasks as well, for example, they could work together to start a school newspaper, or produce a project on something of interest.

Symbols for feedback

It is often useful for learners if you let them make their own corrections to their work. One way of giving learners guided correction is to give them symbols indicating the kind of mistakes they are making. For example, you can use the symbol # when learners make errors of agreement, for example, the third person -s in the present simple, or the letters *sp* when there is a spelling mistake.

ACTIVITY 7

There are some more examples of the kinds of symbols you can use to give learners feedback in the column on the left. Match them with the kinds of mistakes they are highlighting on the right.

sp   word order
wo re-phrase
ww number / concord (for example, verb-noun agreement)
st   spelling
t   punctuation
p   tense
rp   wrong word
structure

ACTIVITY 8

Look at the letter below and correct it using the symbols above or your own equivalents.

Dere Martin

I hope you are well I am well.

I am came to see you yesterday. But you are out. Please to telephone to me when you can. I will have a party in wednesday and I want that you come. There will be much funs at the party.

I hope really you can come.

Maurizio

PORTFOLIO WORK

List three types of writing that your learners might need to do or would enjoy doing. How would you prepare them to write the text types? Can you think of three activities for each text type: one in which they prepare to write, one in which they produce a first draft and then one in response to feedback? For example, if you think they often write emails to each other, you could look at a model email, and identify how it is structured (for example, does it begin with Dear …, and how does it end?). You could then get your learners to write their own emails using the text as a model. Feedback could be done by peer correction.

Layout

Put together a sample, for example, of a formal letter, and cut out the various elements:

– sender's address
– date
– receiver's name and address
– opening salutation ('Dear Ms. …,')
– opening paragraph
– main paragraph
– closing paragraph
– closing salutation ('Yours sincerely, …')

Make copies of the cut-outs and give them to pairs or small groups to put back together.

Formality

As we saw on pages 90–91 one way to raise learners' awareness of levels of formality is to compare formal and informal texts.

Study skills

Classes can be given handouts which help them to structure their note-taking. For example, the handout below was given to a group of learners who had to write a report about ways of improving their school canteen. As a follow-up activity, they could then write a letter to the head teacher in which they gave their ideas for change.

Your group has been asked to write a letter to the head teacher listing ways of improving the school cafeteria. Look at the following and make notes under each heading. You do not need to write in full sentences.

Food	*(fast, healthy, gourmet, global)*
Drink	*(soft drinks/water/milk/hot drinks)*
Opening hours	*(breakfast / lunchtime only)*
Type of furniture	*(modern/plastic)*
Layout	*(where the tables and chairs go)*
Décor	*(colour of walls, lighting…)*
Posters or paintings	
Music	

Writing as part of the language learning process

As we saw on page 87 writing is an important part of learning vocabulary, functions, and grammar. Here are some ideas for activities in these three areas:

Vocabulary – lexical sets
In the activity below the learners have been introduced to a lexical set including farm animals, wild animals, and pets. It is helpful for learners to note words in a context or full sentence.

Complete these sentences:

1 A _____ sleeps during the winter.
2 An _____ has a very long trunk.
3 _____ , _____ and _____ are cats.
4 _____ and _____ are farm animals.
5 You can ride a _____ and a _____ .

Vocabulary – collocations

There are no rules for collocations, so they need to be recognized and noted down as they arise. The activity below is one way in which we can make learners aware of collocations. Learners are asked to match the verbs on the left with the nouns they usually go with on the right. For example, we usually talk about '*doing* the housework', but '*making* a cake'.

do	the bed
boil	the shopping
get off	a coat
put on	a book
write	a kettle
make	a plane

PORTFOLIO WORK

It is not just verbs and nouns which collocate. Certain adjectives are often associated with certain nouns. We talk about 'strong' or 'weak' coffee, for example. Devise an activity for your learners which helps them notice the ways in which certain words go together.

This can be a matching activity similar to the one above, or something else – a gap-filling activity, for example. You can focus on verbs or nouns.

Functions

Learners can be given a number of questions which help them to complete the text. For example, here are some questions to help fill in a gapped invitation form:

– What is your name?
– What is the name of the person you are inviting?
– What sort of party is it?
– What day is the party?
– Where is the party?
– What time does the party start?
– What time does it finish?
– Does your guest need to reply?
– Who does your guest need to reply to?

Dear _____

I am having a _____ party on _____ .
Please come to _____ from _____ to
_____ .

Please let me know if you will be coming.

My telephone number is _____

Lots of love,

_____

Grammar

When teaching grammar you may also ask your learners to write things down so that they have time to reflect on the grammar pattern they are trying to learn, and so that you can check on their understanding. The following example is typical of the type of grammar activity used to help elementary learners choose between the singular or plural forms of the verb 'have'.

> Write sentences from these notes. Choose 'has' or 'have' as the verb in each case. The first one has been done for you.

1 I / breakfast / 7 a.m.   I have breakfast at 7 a.m.
2 He / coffee / 11 a.m.   _____
3 They / lunch / 1 p.m.   _____
4 We / tea and biscuits / 3:30 p.m.   _____

LEARNERS' WRITING PORTFOLIOS

Just as you collect together your ideas and experiences and sample activities in your portfolio, so it is a good idea for learners to collect together all their writing in a book, or a file, in a similar way. In this way both you and the learners will be able to monitor their progress. They will be able to look back on their early work, where perhaps they could only write one or two sentences, and compare this with their work later in the year when they could write whole paragraphs. You can also use these portfolios to assess your learners' writing ability over the year. How you decide to organize these portfolios, and what you ask learners to include in them is up to you. Learners could also be allowed to choose three (or more) pieces of work which they think are their best, for formal grading by the teacher.

Summary

Writing skills can be practised both as a set of sub-skills at sentence level and as a process involving a combination of skills at extended text level. The teacher should be aware of the skills that their learners need to develop.

These can be divided into those skills that the learners are weak at and those areas that they will need outside the classroom – for everyday life, their studies, or work. The teacher should base decisions about what activities to introduce on the perceived needs of the learners.

Case study

Go to the 'Case study' section at the back of the book and listen to a teacher talk about their experiences of teaching writing.

8 PLANNING

In this chapter we explore aspects of:

– lesson planning
– a three-stage lesson
– putting together a sequence of lessons
– planning a course.

Lesson planning

Before we teach a lesson we need to decide:

– what the goals or aims of the lesson are
– what resources to use: a coursebook or textbook, **handouts** or **worksheets**, posters, recorded material, etc.
– whether to adapt the coursebook, if we are using one – to supplement, leave out, or replace activities and materials to make them more appropriate for our learners and our teaching methods
– which types of activities the learners will do
– how the learners will interact with you and each other
– the sequence of activities
– the timing and pacing
– how best to use the classroom.

Aims

The aims of a lesson will depend on a number of factors:

– the learners' level: are they elementary, lower intermediate, etc.?
– the class profile: are the learners generally homogeneous or are they a mixed ability class?
– their needs: what new language do they need? what language do they need to practise? Needs can be described in terms of individual needs (what learners need in terms of their own personal development), and institutional needs (what they need to cover in terms of a school or national curriculum and to pass examinations, etc.) (See page 121 for details of **diagnostic tests**.)
– what type of learners are they, for example, visual, kinaesthetic, auditory, and so on (see pages 8 and 9)?

– their interests: what sort of topics interest them?
– their motivation: what sort of activities, topics, or materials motivate them?
– the number of learners: is it a big or small class? how will this affect the types of activities and preparation of materials?
– attendance: do the learners attend regularly?
– assumed knowledge: what have the learners already studied? how well can they recall and use language they have studied?
– anticipated problems: for example, are the learners' abilities mixed? are there any discipline problems?

Language aims

As we have seen, language is usually broken down into three areas – vocabulary, functions, and grammar – and a lesson can focus on one area or cover a mixture of all three.

Skills aims

We have looked at the four skills – listening, reading, speaking, and writing in detail in chapters 4 to 7. When we plan a lesson we need to decide which skills the learners need to practise. We also need to consider the sub-skills. For example, if we have decided to practise reading we need to choose whether to focus on skimming, scanning, reading for detail, and so on.

Subsidiary aims

Some teachers like to include these in their plans. These are the language or skills that your learners practise but which you are not specifically concentrating on in the lesson.

The aims will determine the types of activity, sequence, and resources you use. See the example lesson on pages 109 to 112.

Resources

Resources are anything that we use in the classroom to support the learning process. These include paper-based resources, for example, a coursebook, text, handouts, posters, exercise books, small cards, and so on; recorded material on cassette, CD, DVD, video tape; **realia**, i.e. real objects from outside the classroom such as magazines, packaging, tickets, etc. The choice of resources will depend on availability, cost, and your time.

ACTIVITY 1

Make a list of some more resources that you use in the classroom. What could they be used for in terms of a language or skills lesson?

Coursebooks

There are various ways in which you might need to change things in a coursebook. You might need to add an activity if you think a structure or other language item needs further practice. Sometimes an activity or material may not be appropriate for your learners' particular situation. You may want to change the order in which the activities are done, or even in which the lessons are taught. It is helpful to let your learners know if you are going to omit things or change the order of activities or chapters and explain why you are doing so.

PORTFOLIO WORK

Look back at a coursebook you have used recently. Which activities did you change, if any? What were your reasons for changing or not changing them?

Activities

These can be divided into activities that require the learners to read, write, speak, or listen, or a combination of some or all of these. See chapters 4 to 7.

Skills are often combined in an activity. For example, the learners read a text, answer questions about it, discuss it, then write their own text.

Some activities involve the learners in movement of some kind, for example, dancing, moving hands or legs, moving around the classroom. Other activities involve manipulating objects, for example, choosing items, colouring items, cutting things up, making something, matching items, or ordering items.

ACTIVITY 2

Make a list of some more activity types.

Interaction

The teacher and learners can interact with each other in a wide variety of ways. Here are some examples of **interaction patterns**:

– teacher to whole class
– teacher to individual learner in open class
– teacher to individual learner
– learner to learner in open class
– pair work, i.e. two learners working together
– group work, for example, the class divided into two halves or small groups of three or four
– mêlée: learners move around the class and interact at random.

You may also choose to give the learners time to work on their own. This gives them time to make or review notes, plan, think about what they have studied, and think of any questions they want to ask.

Teacher's position
Think about where you are going to stand and move around. Here are some choices:

– stay at the front of the classroom in front of the board
– walk around the class at random
– if the class is in a semi-circle, walk round from left to right or right to left
– stand at the back of the class.

ACTIVITY 3

Think of some reasons why you would stand in one place or move around.

Types of questions
You need to plan the kind of questions you are going to ask and who you're going to ask. **Open questions** allow the learner to put together an extended answer, for example, 'What did he do at the weekend?' – 'He met his friends in town.' Open questions start with 'What', 'Where', 'Who', 'Why', 'When', and 'How'. 'How' often comes with words such as 'far', 'big', 'much', 'long', 'many', 'heavy', and so on.

Closed questions limit the possible type of answer. Yes/No questions limit the answer to 'Yes' or 'No'. For example, 'Did you go swimming at the weekend?' – 'Yes'. The answer could also include the question verb, in this case 'Yes, I did.' These types of questions start with the **auxiliary verbs** 'be', 'have', or 'do' and **modal verbs** such as 'can' 'should' 'may', and 'will'. Either/or questions limit the choice of answer to two, for example, 'What did he do at the weekend: play football or go shopping?' – 'He went shopping.' True/False questions also limit the choice of answer to two, for example, 'He went shopping at the weekend: True or false?' – 'True'.

Teachers should think about the type of questions and the way they ask them as they affect the learning process in important ways.

ACTIVITY 4

How do the question types described affect the learners in terms of how much and what they say? How do the following questions affect the learners' participation in the lesson:

1 What's this [teacher waits] anyone?
2 What's this [teacher waits] Maria?
3 Maria, what's this?
4 What's this? [teacher waits] Yes, Maria.

Sequence of activities

Lessons with a particular aim are made up of a sequence of activities which relate to each other. We can divide the sequence up into three stages: opening, middle, and end. These three stages are discussed in more detail below.

Timing and pacing

This is determined by how long each lesson is and how much time you have over a term or course. Decide how long each activity will take. A lesson needs to have lots of variety and the pace should be relatively quick for young learners – each activity should be relatively short. Activities can be longer for young adults and adults.

Classroom

The size and shape of the classroom will also affect your lesson plan. Can the learners move around? Is there space for the learners to do physical activities, get into groups, walk around, etc.? How is the furniture arranged? Can it be moved? Some ways of arranging desks in a classroom are shown below.

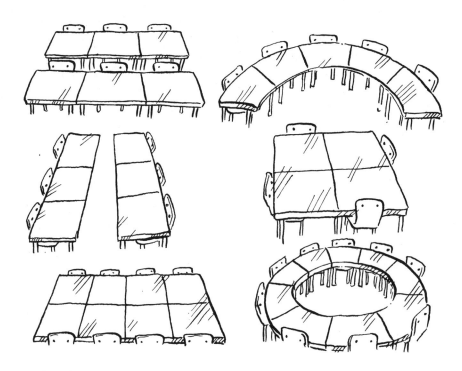

A lesson in three stages

It is useful to break down a lesson plan into three stages: the opening, the middle, and the end. An example of a lesson plan is given at the end of this section which illustrates the points made below.

Opening

In the first part of a lesson the teacher should explain to the learners:

– what the aims of the lesson are
– how the lesson links to previous one(s)
– what activities they are going to do.

Before you start work on a new area it is a good idea to review work that was covered in a previous lesson. This could be done informally by asking the class if they remember what they studied last time, which words, expressions, or structures they remember. It could also be done in a homework checking activity or as a mini-lesson that checks whether the learners can use the language correctly.

You can use a warm-up activity to get the learners' attention and interest. This can be something that is unrelated to the main part of the lesson, for example, a quick 'Simon says' activity (see page 53) or it could be a lead-in to the main part of the lesson.

Middle

This is where you focus on the main aim of the lesson. As we saw in chapter 1, the language learning process can be broken down into five stages:

INPUT ⟶ NOTICING ⟶ RECOGNIZING PATTERNS AND RULE
MAKING ⟶ USE AND RULE MODIFICATION ⟶ AUTOMATING

In the classroom this might involve the learners reading or listening to a text that contains new language. This can be followed by an activity in which the learners focus their attention on this new language. This in turn is followed by an activity that gives them a chance to use the language. (See the account of a PPP lesson in chapter 2.)

For the four skills the main part of a lesson usually focuses on an activity or series of activities that practises one of the skills or sub-skills. In many lessons, as we saw in 'Activities' above, the main part of the lesson is often a combination of activity types.

End

The final part of a lesson aims to bring it to a close or conclusion. There are a number of things you can do in this stage, for example:

– recap the main points of the lesson
– relate the lesson to the goals or aims you stated at the beginning
– show how the lesson links to work done before
– go over any homework instructions or preparation learners must do for the next lesson
– praise learners for what they have achieved in the lesson
– get learners to evaluate the lesson.

A sample lesson plan

Here is a sample lesson plan for a class of 11 to 12 year olds. The plan uses the headings outlined above. You can use this as a model for your own plans and adapt it to fit your class and aims.

Class profile
20 × Russian 11 to 12 year olds; most learners at lower intermediate level, although Goran and Vladimir need a little more help than the others; their spoken English is better than their written English; all learners have some difficulties with the English alphabet; no problems getting them to talk.

Time
60 minutes (twice a week). (Timing is in **bold** in the lesson plan.)

Classroom
Tables are arranged in groups of four; chairs can be moved around. Learners will work with the teacher, in pairs, and in groups. (Interaction sections are underlined.)

Resources
Animal pictures, board, paper and pens for each learner, large sheet of plain paper for each group, reading text, exercise books. (These are in *italics*.)

Aims
To give learners more exposure to and an opportunity to use animal vocabulary, prepositions of place, and comparative adjectives.

To practise giving reasons.

Subsidiary aims
To develop negotiation strategies in English.

To revise the alphabet.

Activity sequence

Opening
Settle the children down and remind them to use English to speak to me and each other as much as possible in the lesson. Tell them what we're going to do in the lesson. (**2 minutes**)

Middle
1 Using *flashcards* of animals, elicit animal vocabulary.
Whole class – the learners try to spell the animal names; I write them on the *board*. Brainstorm any other animal names in English.

Put all words on the board. (**5 minutes**)

getting

2 In pairs, the learners write all the animal names down in alphabetical order. Then they select the animals you would find in a zoo and write another alphabetical list of zoo animals. (**8 minutes**)

3 Plan of a zoo on the *board* with ten sections of different sizes for different animals. Whole class – the learners suggest which animals should go in which section and I write in the names. (**2 minutes**)

4 **Class discussion** about the animals, and ways to group them – for example, by country, by type of animal (e.g. big cats), mammals, and reptiles. (**3 minutes**)

5 **In pairs**, the learners copy the plan of the zoo on to *a sheet of paper.*

They must decide which animals they are going to have in their zoo and where they are going to live. Point out that they need to think about:

   – the types of animals people will want to see
   – the size of the sections where the animals will live
   – whether they want to group any particular animals together.
     (**5 minutes**).

6 **Each pair joins with two other pairs to form groups of six, and one group of eight.** They are given a *large sheet of paper* with the zoo outline on it. They must now negotiate a plan for the zoo between the three pairs. (**8 minutes**)

7 **Each group** prepares an oral report to give to the class. The report explains which animals they have chosen and why they have put them in particular sections of the zoo. (**7 minutes**)

8 **Each group** reports to the class on its zoo. Members of the class are encouraged to question the group if they are not clear about its reasons.

After all the groups have presented their zoos, a vote is taken to decide on the best one. (**15 minutes**)

End
Point out some of the language that the learners have been using and tell them that we will be using it again in the next lesson to do a reading comprehension. If there is time, we play a vocabulary game using the names of animals and some of the new vocabulary that they have just seen and heard. (**5 minutes**)

Homework
Write a paragraph describing where they have put their animals in the zoo and why.

Evaluating a lesson
After you have taught a lesson, it is a good idea to evaluate it. Here are some questions you can use.

Lesson aims
Did you achieve some or all of the aims of your lesson? Why, or why not?

Activity sequence
For each activity, make brief notes including the reasons, based on the following:

– It took more time than planned; it took less time than planned; it went as planned.
– Learners enjoyed / didn't enjoy it.
– I enjoyed / didn't enjoy it.
– Learners found it easy/OK/difficult.
– I would change … if I did the activity again.
– Other comments.

Overall comments:

– How did you feel about the lesson in general?
– What was the best part of the lesson? Why?
– What was the least successful part? Why?
– Did learners have any particular difficulties?
– Can you think of ways in which you could address the difficulties you have mentioned? OR
– Give some brief ideas of follow-up work you would do for this lesson.
– Any other comments you would like to add.

A tip on working with lesson plans – be prepared for change

No matter how well planned a lesson is, it can always go differently in the classroom. Here are some of the reasons a lesson may not go according to plan:

— Sometimes learners will take more time or less time for an activity than you thought, because it's more interesting, generative, difficult, etc.
— You or the learners may come up with a new idea for an activity.
— The learners might know more about the language than you anticipated so you have to move on to the middle stage more quickly.
— The learners might know less language than you anticipated so you need to spend more time on the opening stage.
— The learners ask lots of questions which are related to the lesson and are enjoying interacting with you.
— The learners struggle with the skills activity, for example, the listening text is more difficult than you thought and you have to replay the tape/CD several times.

Keep a file, or book, of all your lesson plans

You can look back on previous work when you are planning future lessons, and when you are drawing up tests or activities to assess your learners' progress.

PORTFOLIO WORK

Now it is time for you to put into practice these ideas about planning by preparing your own detailed lesson plan and, if possible, using it in the classroom. You can choose what you would like to do in the lesson. You could design your own activities, or take activities from a textbook, or use a combination. Think about the stages of a lesson, and about what you want your learners to focus on.

The lesson plan that we looked at above is quite detailed, and the one you have just prepared is probably quite detailed too. As a busy teacher you will not have time to plan every lesson in this much detail. Planning like this is useful, particularly when you are first starting to teach English, because it makes you think about *what* you are doing and *why*. More experienced teachers may only need to make brief lesson plans, except when trying something new.

Putting together a sequence of lessons

Not only do we need to plan each lesson, but we also need to think about a sequence of lessons. We need to plan to make sure lessons fit together effectively over a week, a term, or a year.

Previous lesson → **Current lesson** → Next lesson →
Future lessons / course

Language learning is a cyclical process rather than a linear one. This means that the same structure, vocabulary, or function needs to be **recycled** and revised regularly. This cycle of revision and expansion occurs in a single lesson. For example, in the sample lesson plan we looked at before, the animal vocabulary is repeated and reinforced at each stage.

This cyclical process also needs to occur within a sequence of lessons. After the lesson in the sample lesson plan we cannot decide we have 'done' animal vocabulary or any of the other new language in the lesson. These words need to be revised in another lesson. It is also important, however, not to make the lessons boring, so we need to develop and expand on what has been learnt. So, for example, the next lesson after the one in the sample plan might go on to review the prepositions of place, but then move on to dealing with prepositions of movement as well.

Planning a course

In planning a whole course we detail all the things a learner should learn in that period of time. This list is often decided by the institution, depends upon which coursebook is being used, or is determined by the examination the learners are preparing for.

It is a good idea to carry out a **needs analysis** before writing a course outline if possible. As we saw on p.103 this could relate to individual or institutional needs. Learners studying English for Specific Purposes (ESP), for example, medicine, will need a particular type of English vocabulary and language to be able to read scientific articles in English, interact with patients, etc. It is important to discover what learners need to study before the course starts.

Once we have found out what the learners' needs are, we can consider what language to include in the syllabus and in what order it should come.

Grammar

Grammar items can be graded by:

– complexity of the form: for example, the present simple, 'I live in Thailand' consists of subject + present simple of the verb + place. The present perfect continuous sentence, 'I have been living in Thailand for ten years.' is a more complex structure: subject + present perfect of 'to be' + present participle + place + time phrase. The form of the conditional sentence, 'I would have lived in Thailand but my husband wanted to move to Hong Kong.' is even more complex and consists of subject + perfect conditional + conjunction + subject + simple past + infinitive + place.

– complexity of the meaning: for example, the sentence, 'I live in Thailand.' is relatively simple. It tells us that the speaker has his home in Thailand at present. 'I have been living in Thailand for ten years.' is more complicated, and we need to understand that the speaker started living in Thailand ten years before and is still there now. The conditional sentence 'I would have lived in Thailand but my husband wanted to move to Hong Kong.' is as complex in its meaning as it is in its form. We need to understand the idea of a hypothetical situation in the past.

– complexity of **concept**: for example, the concept of countable and uncountable items does not occur in many languages and involves an understanding of what can be counted, what can't, and why it can't. For example, rice can be counted in small amounts but not when it is in a pile or bag, but it is referred to as uncountable.

– frequency: how often the grammar item is used

– range: how many situations it can be used in

– similarity to learners' L1

– similarity to structures the learners already know.

ACTIVITY 5

Which of these paired structures would you teach first? Can you give a reason for your decision?

– the present continuous to talk about actions occurring as we speak, for example, 'He's reading a newspaper.' or the present continuous to talk about arrangements, for example, 'I'm meeting John tomorrow morning.'

– the present perfect to talk about a recent event, for example, 'I've cut the grass.' or the present perfect continuous to talk about a recent event, 'I've been cutting the grass.'

Look through any coursebooks you use or have used in the past. Do they agree about the order in which they teach grammatical structures? What differences do you notice?

Functions

Many coursebooks organize their syllabus around a list of **functions**. As we saw in chapter 3, functions tell us what is being done with the language, for example, inviting, offering, and so on, and each function has a variety of exponents. A functional syllabus will be comprised of these functions and exponents which will be **graded** according to their complexity, how commonly they are used, and their usefulness.

ACTIVITY 6

Below you have a list of some functions. Which of them would be suitable for your learners? In what order would you teach them? What are your reasons for choosing this order? Are there any other functions that you would add to this list?

Offering	Would you like …?
	Would you care for …?
	I'd be delighted to offer you …
Suggesting	Let's …
	How about …?
	I suggest that …
Apologizing	Sorry.
	I must apologize for …
	We humbly beg your forgiveness.
Introducing	May I introduce …?
	This is …
	It is my great pleasure to present to you …

Vocabulary

Some syllabuses also list the vocabulary or **lexis** a learner will need. Teachers need to consider how useful the vocabulary is and how difficult it is. Difficulty can be described in terms of what the words refer to. Some words refer to a concrete thing, for example 'bus'. These things may be more or less commonly referred to in everyday speech, i.e. 'bus' is referred to more often than a 'booster rocket'. Some words refer to an idea or concept, for example, 'intelligence'. The idea or concept may be relatively simple – 'big', or more complex – 'existentialism'.

As we have seen, words also occur together in noun or verb phrases. Single words with one syllable are easier to say and remember than noun phrases with multi-syllable words. The meaning of some phrases is simply a combination of the meaning of the words in the phrases, for example, '*pick up* a piece of paper.' Sometimes the relationship is not direct, for example, '*get on with* someone'.

ACTIVITY 7

Look at the following vocabulary and decide which order you would teach the items in and why.

talk back   give a talk   talk to   talk shop

We need to take all these factors into account when we are choosing which vocabulary to include in a course and when to introduce it. Sometimes, particularly with ESP, the usefulness factor will override the difficulty factor, i.e. learners will need vocabulary that is relatively difficult and unusual even though their overall English level may not be very advanced.

Pronunciation

In chapter 3 we looked at a number of aspects of pronunciation or phonology. We noted that we needed to know about individual sounds, word and sentence stress, and connected speech. Some course outlines list the particular pronunciation aspects that need to be focused on throughout the course. Generally pronunciation is something that we need to be constantly aware of throughout a series of lessons.

Skills

In earlier chapters we have looked at ways of teaching the individual skills. In a syllabus we need to be sure that we are practising all of the skills, or those which are most relevant to our learners.

ACTIVITY 8

The table on the next page is part of a course outline. The course is organized around a story about three characters, Bridget, Mark, and Daniel, who live and work in London. Complete the outline by putting the language focus details for grammar (G), vocabulary (V), functions (F), and pronunciation (P) into the gaps in the 'Language focus' section of the course outline.

Language focus details:

- describing people
- past simple
- intonation – rise for questions, fall for decisions
- verb phrases with 'go' – shopping, for a walk, to a show.

PORTFOLIO WORK

Most course outlines list several of the elements listed above. Look through the contents list of any coursebook you are using, or others you have used in the past, and compare them with each other. Note down whether they list grammar, functions, vocabulary, skills, pronunciation, or something else. Do you always follow the order of the outline with your classes, or do you sometimes teach the lessons in a different order? Is there anything you would add to these outlines? (for example, timings, potential problems.)

Course outline

Session	Story		Language focus
19.1	The three characters write a description of what happened at a party in their diary.	G	1. _____
		V	as necessary for the diary entry
		F	–
		P	–
19.2	Bridget asks Mark about who was at the party.	G	past simple questions
		V	tall, chatty, friendly
		F	2. _____
		P	rising intonation
19.3	Conversation at the photocopier at work, talking about the coming weekend	G	'going to', present continuous
		V	3. _____
		F	talking about plans and intentions
		P	showing interest via intonation
20.1	Mark is away on business. Daniel asks Bridget out for the evening. They discuss what kind of films they like. The conversation ends with them deciding to go to the cinema.	G	-ing vs. to… vs. bare infinitive let's; shall we; how about
		V	types of films – thriller, romantic comedy, sci-fi
		F	making suggestions stating a preference
		P	4. _____
20.2	Two mini phone dialogues in which Daniel phones the cinema to ask about times of showings.	G	question patterns
		V	prepositions of time
		F	requests, checking information
		P	weak forms

Course projects for children

Children in particular like to have something concrete they can work towards for the end of a course. Does your school ever put on performances for the parents at the end of the term? You can plan a series of lessons which lead up to such a performance. For example, the children can learn songs for the performance, they can practise the vocabulary they will need, or they can even write their own plays.

Children also like to be able to produce something concrete. A series of lessons can build up to creating a story-book or a poster for the classroom.

Summary

In this chapter we have looked at the things we need to know before planning a lesson, we have looked at a sample lesson plan, and you have devised your own detailed plan. We looked at the idea of a cycle in a sequence of lessons, and at various ways of organizing an outline for a whole course.

Case study

Go to the 'Case study' section at the back of the book and listen to a teacher talk about their experiences of planning.

9 ASSESSMENT AND EVALUATION

In this chapter we are going to explore the topic of assessment and evaluation in terms of:

– ways of assessing learners
– the effects of using **tests**
– preparing tests for your learners
– testing the range of language skills
– how to write progress and achievement tests
– preparing learners for external **examinations**
– using portfolios.

Ways of assessing learners

Assessment is the process of analysing and measuring knowledge and ability, in this case, the learners' knowledge of the language and ability to communicate. Assessment can be done either formally or informally. You probably do some informal assessment in all your lessons – by asking questions you check whether your learners have remembered what you taught them or whether they have understood what you are currently teaching them. Formal assessment is done using tests and examinations.

Placement tests

Placement tests are given to learners at the beginning of a new course. The aim is to determine the range of language learners know and can use so that teachers can place them in the most suitable classes or groups.

Diagnostic tests

Diagnostic tests are designed to provide information about individual learners' strengths and weaknesses in specific areas of the language system, for example, a test could tell us about which phonemes a learner is or isn't able to produce accurately in connected speech. This information can be used to put together a study plan or syllabus.

Progress tests

Progress tests are given to learners during a course to see how far their language ability has developed, for example, what vocabulary they can use that they couldn't at the beginning of a course. This can help the teacher judge what needs to be covered in the following section of the course and which parts of the syllabus or coursebook should be revisited.

Achievement tests

Achievement tests are given to learners at the end of the course and are based on what they have studied during the course. They aim to show what learners are able to do at the end of the course that they couldn't do at the beginning of the course, for example, understand a wider range of spoken English, read short, simple texts, make simple requests, and so on.

External proficiency examinations

External proficiency examinations may be produced by the Ministry of Education in a particular country, or by an organization which sets language examinations internationally. These examinations are taken by learners from many different institutions and perhaps from many different countries. Learners often need to do well at these examinations in order to get a particular job or to obtain a place at a university or college.

The most widespread international English language examinations are TOEFL (Test Of English as a Foreign Language), IELTS (International English Language Testing System), and the examinations offered by Cambridge ESOL.

ACTIVITY 1

Think about the following questions and how they relate to your own experiences of teaching and testing your learners:

– Which of the five types of language testing are used in the school where you teach?
– Which of the first four types of test do you think you might need to develop for your learners?
– Which external examinations do your learners have to prepare for? Are they locally or nationally produced, or are they international examinations?

Most schools that teach languages use each of these types of test or external examinations to some extent. However, in the rest of this chapter we will focus on the three types that are probably most important for you: progress tests, achievement tests, and external proficiency examinations. You may well have to prepare progress or achievement tests yourself, so we will consider how to do this effectively. You probably won't be involved in writing external proficiency examinations yourself, but may have to prepare your learners for examinations of this kind. We will look at how you can help learners to do well at these examinations.

The effects of using tests

If we want to prepare good tests for our learners and help them to do well in external examinations, it is important to think about the effects which testing can have on teaching and learning.

Testing and evaluation can have a significant influence on how a teacher works with their learners, and also influences how learners learn. Some of the good and bad effects of testing can include:

- In class, teachers only focus on what will be tested.
- Learners only pay attention to what they think they will be tested on.
- Tests can make some learners very nervous and they may not do as well as they could because of this.
- Tests can help teachers identify areas in which their students are having problems.
- Learners need to practise the test types that they will be given. If they do not understand the test format they will not be able to demonstrate what they know.
- Feedback from tests can help learners see what areas they need to focus on.
- If tests are too difficult, learners will become demotivated.

ACTIVITY 2

Read these comments on how tests affect learning and teaching and compare them to you and your learners' experiences:

Doing well in tests helps my learners feel good about their English and motivates them to learn more.

When my learners make mistakes in tests, it shows me which things I need to revise with them in future lessons.

My learners hate tests. They get very nervous and the atmosphere in the class changes.

Lots of my learners only really start to work well when they know they've got to do a test soon.

Tests often concentrate too much on accuracy rather than on fluency or communication skills.

External examinations make us waste time practising silly exam questions. It would be more useful to be talking or reading than practising exam techniques.

Lots of external examinations don't pay enough attention to speaking, which is what my learners really need most.

> Working towards an exam gives us all a specific goal. We all know exactly what we have to do and learners and teachers are united by the shared aim of doing as well as we can and getting good marks.

Preparing tests for your learners

The following guidelines should help to make progress and achievement tests a positive experience for your learners.

Test what you have taught

It is important for progress and achievement tests that you only test what you have previously taught and can expect your pupils to know. In this way all your pupils have an equal chance of being successful, which will help to build their confidence. This means also that you need to pay attention to the language used in a test. For example, new vocabulary or new grammatical structures should not appear for the first time in a test.

Test what is useful

For example, if your learners have studied asking for things in a shop using 'Could I have … please?', tell them to 'Ask for an apple in a shop', rather then tell them to 'Write a request using 'could'.

Test all four skills

It may seem easier to prepare grammar and vocabulary tests. But the four skills are all important and they involve more than just a knowledge of grammar and vocabulary. We will explore ways in which you can test each of the skills later in this chapter.

Tell your learners 'when' and 'what'

If you tell your learners that you are going to give them a test, make sure they are able to revise what they have learnt. Revising for a test helps learners learn and remember what they have been taught. It also means that they are not surprised when they are given a test, so they are not nervous and do better.

Make sure the instructions are clear

Include an example and use your learners' L1 if necessary. Remember, you are testing your learners' English skills, not how good they are at doing tests. Check that learners understand what they have to do by giving them the opportunity to ask questions before the test starts. This is particularly important with learners who have not done a particular type of test before, or learners who are very young and might not remember the instructions from an earlier occasion.

Make use of materials that are already available

The course materials you use with your learners may include progress tests. If not, you can adapt exercises from the other books your learners are using and turn them into classroom tests. In the next section we consider some ways of doing this.

Types of tests

The following types of test involve a number of different aspects of language use. Testing experts agree that they are all good ways of testing learners' language knowledge. They are all simple to prepare and it is easy to base them on work your learners have been doing. As a teacher you can prepare these for use with your own classes, or for institutional examinations you might need to produce. It is also important that you are familiar with them in order to prepare your learners for examinations which might contain them.

Dictation

Dictation is a very good way of testing listening and writing skills. You can easily make a short dictation by using part of a text that your learners have already read or listened to. Read the whole text through once. Then dictate it phrase by phrase. Then read it through one more time. When the learners have checked their texts, ask them to read the text back to you or hand them in to be marked.

Gap-fill tests

A gap-fill test is a text in which individual words are missing. Learners have to fill in the missing words. Try the following example for yourself.

> Gap-fill tests are said to be very good tests of a learner's language ability. These tests are texts where words _____ missed out. Learners have _____ fill in the missing words. When you are preparing these tests, _____ should make sure you only miss _____ words which learners can work out, _____ example, prepositions, articles, auxiliary verbs, or pronouns.

You can make these tests from reading or listening texts in materials you use with your learners. If you are studying a particular grammar or vocabulary area, you can select which words to remove to encourage your learners to think about the area you are studying. You might decide only to remove the adjectives or question words, for example. A variation of this type of test makes it a little easier. Learners are given an alphabetical list containing the words that have been removed from the text, and about five additional words. The following words are from the example text, with three additional words.

are	you	out	have
am	on	for	to

C-tests

In a C-test the second half of every second word is missing. Learners have to complete the words. Try the following example:

> C-tests give learners more clues about the words they have to write. It
> i_____ therefore poss_____ to mi_____ out a wi_____ variety
> o_____ different kin_____ of wor_____ .

C-tests often involve several short texts so that a wider variety of language is tested. They typically require learners to complete 40–50 words. Notice that both gap-fill tests and C-tests give learners a complete first sentence so that they know what the text is about.

Multiple-Choice Questions

Multiple-choice questions are a common type of test and can be used to test both individual language items, such as vocabulary or grammar, or listening or reading comprehension. A multiple-choice question usually gives the learner a choice of one correct answer and two or three incorrect ones, for example:

> I always take my umbrella when I …
> a have gone for a walk.   ☐
> b went for a walk.   ☐
> c go for a walk   ☐

The incorrect answers in a multiple choice question are called **distractors**. Sometimes a multiple choice question test will have one distractor that is clearly wrong but another that is almost right in order to make the learner think carefully before answering. Again, they can be written to focus on a range of aspects of language.

Word order

Putting the words into a random order makes the learners think about sentence construction and the relationship between words, phrases, and clauses. Obviously, the longer and more complex the sentence the more difficult the test, for example:

> watching I reading and like TV.
> director I am to John, who going used to meet be a film.

Sentence completion

Many tests require learners to complete sentences with an appropriate word or phrase. Learners can be given a choice of answers or a prompt, for example, the infinitive of the verb needed:

> I _____ (have been, went) to Australia three times. The first
> time was when I was child. I _____ (to go) to Australia three
> times. The first time was when I was a child.

Sentence transformation

This is the name given to tests where the learner has to complete a second sentence so that it means the same as a sentence already given. This kind of test is often used to assess how well learners know how to use the passive and reported speech.

> The man bit the dog.
> The dog ——————— the man.
>
> Doctor: 'You need to go to the hospital.'
> The doctor said that ——————— .

ACTIVITY 3

When producing a gap-fill activity, it is important that you have a reason for your choice of which items to remove. Usually the reason is because you want to focus on a particular language area. Look at the short text below and decide which words you would remove if you were removing all the articles, adjectives, and adverbs.

> The postman where I live is very old. He walks slowly and often delivers the letters very late. The people in my street are happy with this because he is also very friendly and has delivered our letters for many years. Every time you meet him, he gives you a big smile and a wave. He knows the name of everybody in the street so if the address is unclear on a letter or a parcel, he always knows which house it is for.

ACTIVITY 4

Answer the three test questions below and decide which grammar points each question is testing:

1 Select the correct form of the verbs given to complete the following sentence:

> While I ——————— (was having/had) a bath, the telephone
> ——————— (ring, rang).

2 Complete the following sentences by putting the verb given into the correct form and using any additional words given appropriately:

> I ——————— (to finish, just) the report my boss ——————— (to ask) me to write yesterday.

3 Complete the second sentence so its meaning is the same as the first:

> A thief stole my car.
> My car ———————

Now write a question of your own to test the same language points using the same type of tests.

PORTFOLIO WORK

Make three short tests for your learners selected from those listed above. Base
your tests on texts from books you use with your learners. You can use the texts
for dictations, gap-fill exercises, C-tests, or for reading comprehension. Choose
grammar points or vocabulary you have already taught for any sentence
transformation or sentence completion exercises. You can use multiple choice
questions for comprehension activities or to test vocabulary or grammar. For each
test, decide which learners you would use it with and what language items it tests.
Keep the tests you prepare in your portfolio.

Testing the range of language skills

It is important to assess all your learners' language skills and not just their use
of grammar or vocabulary. The different language skills can be tested in
many different ways. Here are four examples:

Testing listening skills

I sometimes give my pupils a short dictation of a few sentences, using
vocabulary they know. Or I may get them to listen to a short dialogue and
answer some questions on it. I usually give them at least two opportunities to
listen to the dictation or dialogue. The dialogue may be on audio cassette, or
role played by me and a pupil, or role played by two learners in the class.

Another task I use is to give pupils a copy of a simple map. They have to draw
a route on it following my directions, for example, 'walk past the church and
turn right by the hairdresser's', or they have to find a destination following
my directions.

Testing speaking ability

I usually do pair work to test my pupils' speaking ability. This tests their
listening as well. Doing pair work helps them feel more relaxed about being
tested. Sometimes I give a pair of learners a picture to talk about. They ask
each other questions about the picture and discuss things they can see in it.

I also use problem-solving tasks with pairs of learners. For example, I give
them pictures of a number of different people, and some pictures of different
presents. Their task is to decide which present to give to each person. They
are not allowed to use a present more than once.

Other examples of pair work would be making learners do role plays or talk
about particular topics. I make sure that I focus on how fluent learners are,
how well they interact with each other, and how effectively they communicate. I don't worry too much about how accurate my learners are in grammar

and pronunciation. If I want my pupils to give me longer answers when I ask them a question, I am careful to use open rather than closed questions.

Testing reading

When I want to test reading comprehension, I try to start with broader questions which focus on the main ideas of a text, for example: 'Is this text about (a) sport, (b) travel, (c) careers?' I then add questions which ask for specific information from the text, but of course I don't expect students to focus on unimportant details.

Sometimes, I only test their ability to skim a text for the main ideas – for example, I might ask them to look at the front page of a newspaper and write down what the main stories are about. At other times I will ask students to scan a text for specific information – for example, to look at some entertainment information in a newspaper and to find out which films are showing on a particular evening.

Testing writing

I have found that my pupils generally don't do as well at writing tasks that they have to do in a set period of time in class. This isn't surprising because they don't have much time to come up with ideas and to write them down in a well-planned way. For this reason I often tell them in advance what I am going to ask them to write about. I may give them help with ideas, for example, by asking them to describe their morning routine, and giving them a series of pictures of people waking up, getting dressed, eating breakfast, and so on.

Sometimes I let the children do their writing tests at home. I tell them that they can use dictionaries and grammar books but that they shouldn't ask anyone else to help them. (I can always tell if they have had help!)

When I mark their writing, I try to look first for positive things – good expressions which they have used, interesting ideas which they have communicated, good organization into clear paragraphs. Sometimes it is too easy just to notice their spelling and grammar mistakes, and that makes both me and my learners feel bad about their work.

PORTFOLIO WORK

Think of three more ideas for each type of skills test, for example, for listening:

> Give the learners the lyrics of a song with some words missing. Play the song and ask them to write down the missing words.

Integrated skills testing

As well as testing language skills separately, it is possible to test them together in an integrated way. Often testing skills in this way is closer to the way the skills will be used outside the classroom. For this reason integrated skills testing is often considered more communicative and more like using language in real life.

Preparing learners for external examinations

Make sure you know exactly what your learners have to learn for the examination, and what they have to do in the examination. You should get a copy of the examination syllabus and some past exam papers. This information should help you plan your course so that you gradually introduce your learners to the language and skills tested in the examination, and to the types of question used. Balance the time spent on past examination papers with other course work.

When you use class time to prepare for an examination, don't focus just on the examination, but use it as an opportunity to give learners useful language practice. If your learners see the language as useful, they are more likely to enjoy the lessons and remember what they have studied.

It is a good idea to give your learners a 'mock exam' a month or two before they take their real exam. If possible, use a recent past paper for this, so that it is as close as possible to the real exam. Knowing exactly what they have to do and how much time they have to do it will help the learners' confidence.

Lots of learners lose marks in exams by doing silly things. Some simple, practical matters can make a big difference to their marks. You can help your learners a lot by training them to:

– read the questions carefully
– do exactly what they are asked
– keep an eye on the time and give only a certain amount of time to each question
– attempt all the questions they are supposed to attempt
– check their answers
– make any corrections as neatly as possible
– write or speak clearly.

Using portfolios

A **portfolio** is a collection of a learner's work and can be used instead of a test to assess how well a learner is doing. The advantage of the portfolio as a means of assessment is that it does not rely on how well the learner performs on a single day, as a test or examination does, but looks at their work over a period of time (see Figure 9.1).

A portfolio usually includes written work, drawings, tests, teacher's notes, self-assessment forms, and so on. Because each portfolio is different it means that each learner is being assessed individually on their own merits. Rather than being something imposed from outside, portfolios are learner-centred and collaborative. This encourages the learner to become more involved in the learning process and develop an awareness of how to assess their own progress.

Portfolio review

Name ___Alice___   Class ___2___   Term ___Spring___

Area	Overall achievement	Strengths	Needs and future action
Reading	Very good	– Loves books and reads a lot. – Uses pictures and context to understand unknown words.	– Needs to improve her reading speed and learn to read silently. – Should continue with readers during holidays.
Writing	Good	– Her handwriting and spelling have improved.	– Has a few problems with combining sentences. – Should practise writing short paragraphs (2–3 sentences).
Speaking	Good	– Always eager to use English. – Can talk about herself and her daily activities.	– Fluency hampered by frequent gaps in vocabulary. – Should try to increase her vocabulary.
Listening	Very good	– Can easily grasp main idea/gist of a listening text.	– Does not always recognize spoken form of words in her vocabulary. – Try listening to tapes of stories with the book open.
Attitude to English	Excellent	– Loves learning English and is always enthusiastic about her lessons.	

Teacher's signature _____   Child's signature _____

Parent's signature _____

Figure 9.1 A portfolio review (from Assessing Young Learners*)*

Summary

Assessment plays an important part in the learning process, both as a motivational factor for the learners and as a tool for the teacher. Tests need to be carefully designed and implemented to ensure that they are a positive factor in the learning process and an accurate indication of learners' abilities which informs the teacher's decisions regarding what and how to teach.

Case study

Go to the 'Case study' section at the back of the book and listen to a teacher talk about their experiences of assessment.

CASE STUDIES

Here are nine case studies from real teachers talking about real teaching and learning situations around the world. Each case study contains a teacher's account of their experience and opinions relating to topics which have been raised in the previous chapters in the book. You can listen to the CD, read the transcripts, or follow both at the same time. There are questions about the case study and an activity at the end of each section. The answers are in the 'Answer key'.

[N.B. The teachers are represented by voice actors.]

Chapter 1
Learning and teaching English ALASTAIR DOUGLAS

Alastair Douglas has been working in ELT since 1997. He has taught both young learners and adults in Japan and Indonesia. Since 2001 he has been working as a teacher and teacher trainer at International House in London.

What did you know about teaching before you began your training course? Did you find the course helpful?
I didn't know quite what to expect when I turned up on my first day for teacher training. In actual fact I found the course a very intensive and fairly enlightening experience and looking back on it a few years later there are a number of parts that do particularly stand out in my memory.

What do you remember best about the course?
One thing that stands out in my mind most of all is the foreign language lesson – it was something that I hadn't really experienced before. I had learnt languages when I was at school but these were taught in a traditional way with lots of grammar and translation. When I was taught Japanese in my teacher training course I was taught entirely through the medium of Japanese. There was no translation and it was a language that I had no idea about. I didn't know what to expect but I was still able to pick up some useful phrases and language in a very short space of time.

Was there anything else on the course that you found particularly useful?
The other thing that I found useful from the training course was being given a number of different basic frameworks of how to present language or deal with receptive skills – like listening and reading, that is. We were given a fairly basic checklist for all sorts of different methods of presenting language.

By following these basic rules I certainly lost a lot of my fear of teaching because I knew that I could fall back on this basic training.

These patterns have followed me right through to this day, some of the basic things like getting students to compare answers before giving feedback, setting tasks before giving handouts, or pre-teaching any difficult vocabulary before getting students to read a text. They are so engrained in my memory that these days they come as second nature.

How do you think we as teachers can help students learn a language?
I think some of the initial problems that students have in learning a language come about when they don't know what to expect, they don't know what to do, and they don't really know why they are being asked to do certain things in class. So I think actually we can make a lot more progress with students if we tell them why we are getting them to do things and why they are doing things in a particular way. I think this does help enormously.

What sort of problems do you think language learners can have?
I think one of the problems that students have is that they worry about getting things wrong. In fact I think we need to make it quite clear to students that we are there to help them improve their language and that making mistakes is part of the learning process.

I think another of the big problems students have with learning a language is their desire to translate everything. The danger of this is that as a result students formulate the sentences in their own language in their mind and then try to translate them into English. This sometimes means that the language often comes out in a very awkward fashion, because translation is actually a very difficult skill. In my experience one of the best ways of improving language learning is to get learners away from the idea of translating and getting them into the idea of formulating sentences in English in their own mind.

How has your own teaching changed in the years since you did your training course?
In terms of how my teaching has perhaps developed since I took my teacher training course, one thing I can say is that I have actually gone through different phases. When I first started teaching I just followed the rule book as I mentioned earlier, then I went through a phase of experimenting with much more complex ways of teaching, and I would say now I've probably gone back to being simpler again. Some of the methods of teaching, such as task-based learning and the lexical approach, were not really around when I was taught to be a teacher and it was very much a PPP type model that we followed with a strong emphasis on teaching lots of grammar. I have now moved away from teaching so much grammar – I don't avoid it, but I don't see the necessity of teaching a great deal of complex grammar.

So what do you focus on these days?
My main emphasis these days is on teaching vocabulary or more particularly, chunks of language, and I have found that actually this has produced much more effective results. I mainly focus on giving students new language they can use directly rather than going into complex grammatical constructions. So I give them words, chunks of language, collocations, or fixed and semi-fixed phrases. I have often tried to do this through texts – both written and spoken – because I think this tends to put the language in context for the students.

Are there some things that you learnt on your teacher-training course which you still find useful?
Of course a lot of the basic frameworks do still apply and I do still follow the same sorts of methodologies. So for example, I still make sure I get the students' interest before they read something, I pre-teach any difficult vocabulary, giving students a gist task before reading. So I still rely on these real basics in my teaching. A lot of the basic nuts and bolts that I was taught on my teacher training course are still completely relevant to the way I teach and I hope have helped me to be a relatively successful teacher.

QUESTIONS

1 Match the following phrases on the left from Alastair's account of his experiences of learning and teaching languages with their explanations on the right:

   – pick up   listening and reading
   – receptive skills   guide to the things you need to do
   – checklist   be memorable
   – stand out   learn

2 Complete the sentences with the correct preposition from the list below. There is one extra preposition that you do not need.

   back   up   out   of

   A Alastair didn't know what to expect when he turned _____ for his teacher-training course.
   B When he looks _____ on the experience now he thinks the course was useful.
   C His experience of learning Japanese through the medium _____ Japanese was one of the most interesting parts of the course.

3 Complete the sentences about some of the basic aspects of teaching that Alastair mentions by matching the phrases on the left with the correct endings on the right:

   – Get learners to check their answers   before giving out handouts
     with each other

     – Pre-teach vocabulary   before giving feedback
     – Set a task   before learners read a text

4 Which of the following does Alastair NOT mention as a problem for learners of a foreign language?

    A fear of making mistakes
    B not wanting to speak in class
    C translating everything into their own language
    D not knowing why they are doing a particular activity

5 Which of the following teaching methods does Alastair NOT mention?

    A PPP
    B task-based learning
    C lexical approach
    D audiolingualism

6 Alastair has moved away from teaching a lot of grammar to:

    A getting students to do more translation
    B teaching students set phrases
    C using only English in class

7 Alastair uses texts in his teaching because:

    A they let the learners see the language in context
    B they are more realistic
    C learners can practise both reading and speaking skills through texts

8 Which of the following does Alastair NOT mention he does before a reading task?

    A giving learners a skimming activity
    B pre-teaching vocabulary
    C giving learners a gist activity

ACTIVITY

Read through Alastair's account of his teaching experience and practice. In what ways do you think he fulfils the characteristics of an effective teacher as listed on pages 3 and 4 of Chapter 1?

Chapter 2
Methodology JAN MADAKBAS

Jan Madakbas is a teacher and teacher trainer. He has worked as Director of Studies and teacher trainer in Moscow and as a teacher in Istanbul. He has experience of teaching a broad range of levels and nationalities, and is also a Cambridge examiner.

What did you know about language teaching before you did any training to be a teacher, for example, from your own language learning experience?

Before I started my teacher-training course I had no idea about methodology at all. All I knew was that when I was at school we did a lot of listening and repeating in my French and German lessons. We learnt about grammar rules, the rules were written on the board in English and we were then supposed to write them down. In the French classes we would listen and repeat, listen and repeat, and we used to read aloud as well. I don't know how useful that was, but certainly I could recognize a word and say it.

Were there any particular types of lessons or activities that you found helpful in your own language learning experience?

What I probably found most helpful was my school trip to Germany. It involved total immersion since I didn't meet anyone who spoke any English and I had to speak German all the time. There was a real need to communicate – unless I said the right sort of things then no one would understand me, and I would have to get it right. So using the language in a real way meant I learnt a lot and by the end of the two weeks I was actually thinking in German.

Now on training courses a lot of people talk about having real-life tasks, tasks which reflect what goes on in the world outside the classroom. So, for example, negotiating with a sales person might be a real thing you want to emulate in the classroom, so you would be practising all sorts of language that would be necessary in that kind of situation. The idea that practice in the classroom is a rehearsal for real life outside the classroom is one that I find a good guide.

What did you learn about methodology in your training course? For example, did you learn about specific methods such as task-based learning, or ways of structuring a lesson such as presentation, practice, and production?

When I was on my teacher-training course I was taught to present, to practise, and to give freer practice afterwards. Unlike the French and German classes I had, teachers these days give students the chance to speak more freely and not just in drills. At the same time I do think students need feedback and correction at the end of freer practice activities. One of the things I find very useful is to walk around the class listening to the freer practice and to make a note of the most frequent errors, the errors that get in the way the most. I focus on them at the end of the class and get students to offer corrections. So I would write the sentences with the mistakes in on the board and then I would say, all these examples have got mistakes in, in pairs, try to find the mistakes and correct them. Sometimes I will underline a mistake in red to just help them along the way. After that we would have student and teacher feedback in the usual way with me asking different pairs for their answers and checking to see if everyone agrees.

Despite the fact that these days everyone talks about real life and natural ways of practising, I still think there is space for the more artificial form of practice using drills and repetitions. I always think that students are in class, they know they are in class, and they expect to do some artificial practice. Accuracy is also an important part of learning a language. Students don't really mind doing things which are removed from reality as long as they feel they are learning the language.

What classes do you teach? How would you describe the methods you use in your classes?
At the moment I teach mostly advanced students. With advanced students most of my teaching takes place around a text. It really just means getting them to listen or to read a piece of text, understand it and then focus on the little bits of language in that text. So after we do comprehension, usually what I end up focussing on is collocation. Students are often quite good at individual words but don't really know how they fit together with the rest of English. We focus on expressions rather than single words for the most part. I think this is part of the lexical approach where you treat a particular group of words as a chunk, a unit of meaning. So now they hardly ever focus on single items.

Probably the most important thing about methodology is to be flexible and ready to try out different things. I'm learning all the time.

QUESTIONS

1 Which of the methodologies below comes closest to Jan's experience of learning French and German?

   A audiolingual
   B communicative language teaching
   c task-based learning

2 Total immersion is:

   A speaking the target language for a week
   B reading and writing in the target language
   c hearing, reading, and using only the target language all the time.

3 Complete the sentence below with the most appropriate option.

   The idea that practice in the classroom is a ... for real life is a good one.

   A task
   B rehearsal
   c guide

4 Complete the sentence below with the most appropriate word.

   The teacher feels it is important to give students ... after any freer practice.

A feedback

B presentation

C mistakes

5 The teacher thinks drills and artificial activities can help students with:

A fluency

B real life

C accuracy

6 When dealing with mistakes the teacher often:

A gets the learners to correct their own mistakes

B asks the learners to make the corrections for homework

C writes the correct version on the blackboard

7 With the advanced class the teacher often focuses on collocations. Collocation is:

A looking at small bits of language

B the way in which certain words often occur together

C taking words from a text

8 The teacher talks about looking at a 'chunk' of language. This is:

A looking at a group of words

B looking in detail at single words

C understanding a word from its context

ACTIVITY

Read through Jan's account of his teaching experience and practice. Can you tell what his views are on the five language teaching methods listed at the beginning of Chapter 2?

Chapter 3

Language MARTA PEREZ-YARZA

Marta Perez-Yarza is from Spain. She teaches teenagers from 14 to 17 years old at Sopelana High School and has been a teacher for over twenty years.

Which area of the language do you focus on most with your students, for example, grammar, vocabulary, pronunciation, or functions?
I focus most on functions. In my opinion learning a language means being able to communicate, to exchange oral or written information. In order to do so, grammar, vocabulary, and pronunciation have to be learnt, not as an aim in themselves but as part of a communicative process. I teach at a Secondary school – my students have very often been taught in Primary school by teachers who put more emphasis on grammar and vocabulary. As a result, my students' ability to communicate is often very poor and they have

what I call grammar phobia. Besides, this new generation requires a new teaching approach. They hardly ever memorize anything; they have a very short concentration span, they are used to sitting for a long time in front of screens (the TV, a Play Station, or the computer) and they are used to moving on every time they get bored. I feel that I have to give them a reason to use the language and the best way to do that is by offering them information that interests them, so I use topics linked to real life and from there we focus on learning the necessary grammar structures, vocabulary, or pronunciation.

How do you usually introduce new grammar to your students? Do you generally introduce grammar in the same way or use different methods?
I have a text book, the *Oxford Exchange*, so I try to cover the objectives and contents in that. I follow the order of the grammar points in the book. I don't say to the students we are going to study the present tense but I rather say we are going to talk about habits. I give them models, written or oral. Sometimes they don't know what an adverb is, or the difference between an adjective or a verb, not to mention what the passive voice is. They simply don't care about those classifications. So by listening, in the same way that little children learn how to speak, they start picking up concepts, grammar and vocabulary. It is not easy as in Spain they hear very little spoken English and at their age they don't really feel the need to learn foreign languages. I play it by ear and by intuition. Motivation and concentration are two important factors when you are introducing new grammar points to teenagers. Teaching these points early in the morning is easier than later in the day. So I may use communication games, a song or a music video if it fits my needs. Once I taught the second conditional with a song.

What sort of activities do you give your students to practise vocabulary?
Their tendency is to write long lists of vocabulary which are worth nothing. I try to teach them to record new words grouped by topics, by opposites, for example. I found they learn a lot of vocabulary when we do content-based learning. For example, when the Asian tsunami occurred or Hurricane Katrina hit New Orleans, we used the Internet to find information and they ended up knowing a lot of geographical vocabulary and words related to natural disasters, rescue teams, and survival techniques.

Are there any particular areas of pronunciation that you focus on with your students?
As I said, my students get very little input of spoken English. All films they are likely to see are dubbed in Spanish. I use the suggested pronunciation items in the book but I find that the recordings are often too artificial. At the beginning I don't correct their pronunciation too much so as not to discourage them, but then I put emphasis on some of the sounds that we Spanish people miss consistently, for example, the initial 's', the initial 'h', the soft 'r', the 'sh' or 'th' sound. This year I have put satellite TV in the classroom

so they can listen to real English speakers. I also show them non-dubbed films and, of course, those who like music in English learn good pronunciation much faster.

How important is it for your students to know about and be able to use functional language, for example, requests, invitations, suggestions, and so on?
My students are not used to being polite so I have to start by telling them to say 'Good morning' when they walk into the classroom and make sure they know about the British social conventions. In order to teach a function I try to find a situation that requires that language. So, for example, I usually ask my students to prepare a role play that includes suggestions, plans, and invitations and they have to perform it. We also do role plays involving shopping, ordering at the restaurant, and so on to make sure they learn that basic language.

QUESTIONS

1 Marta thinks that grammar, vocabulary, and pronunciation are:

   A part of the communication process
   B an important element in language learning in themselves
   C not important in learning a language

2 Marta thinks the present younger generation need to be taught differently because they:

   A have learnt too much grammar
   B like to memorize everything
   C they have a short concentration span

3 When she is teaching grammar Marta thinks it is:

   A important that the students know the grammatical terminology
   B not important for the students to know the grammatical terminology
   C not useful for students to learn any grammar

4 Tick the factors that Marta believes are important when new grammar is being introduced:

   a time of day ☐
   b complexity of the function ☐
   c motivation ☐
   d grammatical terminology ☐
   e similarity to the students' own language ☐
   f concentration ☐
   g complexity of the form ☐

5 Marta thinks that a helpful way of teaching vocabulary is to:

   A give students a list of new words
   B give students a context in which they can learn new words
   C teach students to use a dictionary

6 Outside the classroom Marta's students hear:

   A a lot of spoken English
   B very little spoken English
   C a lot of films in English

7 When teaching pronunciation Marta focuses on:

   A correcting all the students' pronunciation errors
   B the recordings from her course book
   C the specific sounds that Spanish speakers find difficult

8 Marta teaches functional language by:

   A finding a situation that uses a particular function
   B giving students a list of expressions for a particular function
   C making sure students are always polite

ACTIVITY

Read through Marta's account of her teaching experience and practice. To what extent do you agree with her views on teaching grammar, vocabulary and pronunciation? Do you teach these elements differently in your own classes?

Chapter 4
Listening SILVANA RAMPONE

Silvana Rampone teaches at the 'Gianni Rodari' primary school in Italy. Her students are aged between 6 to 10. Silvana is a primary EFL teacher, teacher trainer, and e-learning tutor for training programmes developed by the Italian Ministry of Education.

What sort of things do your learners listen to?
As I mainly teach very young learners, I usually get my students to listen to songs, stories, and TV programmes. The Italian Ministry of Education has started a special TV programme that gives children the possibility to watch and listen to sketches and authentic materials in English (educational programmes, cartoons). Students start listening to short dialogues from the age of six and the dialogues are usually related to the text book they use. Moreover, learners listen to stories and songs from the Internet or CD-ROMs.

What sort of listening activities do you do with your students?
The activities depend on the kind of listening material I'm using and on the students' age. If I use songs with very young learners, I choose active songs to let them use vocabulary and structures they already know; new words are made clear through miming or pictures. With older students, I usually get them to listen to the whole song first, then I give them the written text and ask them to underline new words. I introduce new words using pictures or matching games (from the English word to the Italian word). I love telling stories to children and I think that creating the right atmosphere is very important. I use voice pitch and gestures to do this. I try to involve children in the storytelling too. For example, I ask the children to stand in a circle, listen, and mime the story with me while I'm telling it. When we listen to stories from CDs or text books, I prepare pictures of the story in advance and ask children to put them in order while listening to the story or, at the end of the listening time, I ask students to choose only the pictures that refer to the story and put them in the right sequence.

I use a great deal of 'listen and do' activities: listen and mime, listen and draw, listen and match, listen and fill in the gaps, listen and answer the questions, listen and tick 'True' or 'False', listen and follow the instructions, or listen and identify a character.

How often do your students listen to English (apart from the English you use in class)?
Students at primary level don't have many opportunities to listen to English outside the class. They sometimes listen to modern songs, read adverts in English, or watch special children TV programmes in English on the national satellite. Very few of them travel abroad or have friends who speak English or attend English clubs.

What are the main problems for your students when listening to English?
The main problem is a lack of concentration in many students so that they need to listen to the same item more than once. Another problem is that some listening activities are too difficult for students because the language is not at their level or the sound is not clear.

How do you help students with these problems?
I generally help my students by doing a lot of preparation before the listening. So, for example, I introduce new vocabulary before the listening or give a short summary of the content of the listening in their mother tongue. While they are listening I give them a list of things I want them to listen to and be able to report, for example, the number of people speaking, place, time, sounds.

I sometimes give my students a worksheet that they fill in during or immediately after the listening, for example, for a listening about animals I give them a worksheet with a list of animals and the students have to circle only those named in the listening. For a Christmas song, I give them pictures of presents and they have to cross out those that are not in the song while listening to it.

QUESTIONS

1   Tick the things that Silvana mentions which can be used to practise listening with young learners:

a TV programmes ☐   f poems ☐
b songs ☐   g the Internet ☐
c CD-ROMS ☐   h films ☐
d stories ☐   i short dialogues ☐
e cartoons ☐   j announcements ☐

2   Which of the following does Silvana NOT use as a way of explaining new words?

A mime
B pictures
c dictionary
D matching to a translation

3   Silvana creates the right atmosphere for a story by:

A using voice pitch and gestures
B using pictures and gestures
c using mime and gestures

4   Which of the following does Silvana NOT mention as a way of involving children in a story?

A mime
B pictures
c sound effects

5   Complete the sentence with the most suitable word from the list below:

Silvana does a lot of 'listen and ....' activities with her students.

A do
B make
c think

6   Are the following statements true or false?

A Silvana's students hear a lot of English outside the classroom.
B Silvana's students sometimes listen to modern songs.
c Silvana's students all attend English clubs.

7   Silvana thinks the main problem students have with listening is that:

A they don't hear enough English

B they don't concentrate

C English people speak too fast

8 In Silvana's view the best way of helping students with listening is to:

A choose extracts which are clear

B do a lot of preparation with the students before they listen

C choose activities which are easy

ACTIVITY

Read through Silvana's account of her teaching experience and practice. In what ways does Silvana get her learners to practise the various listening skills listed on page 48?

Chapter 5
Speaking MAŁGORZATA KUŁAKOWSKA

Małgorzata Kułakowska has taught English at a secondary school in Kielce in Poland since 1993.

What in your view are the major problems for your students when learning to speak in a foreign language?

The ability to speak a foreign language fluently is seen by most students as a desirable skill but the most difficult one to learn. The problem connected with acquiring it is the proper balance between all the needed sub-skills.

On the one hand, there are students who use English outside the classroom. They are often quite confident about their command of the language especially after talking to non-native speakers. If they are able to communicate with other teenagers in English successfully, they stop worrying about their mistakes and get used to wrong forms. It is not the biggest problem but then it is usually quite difficult to encourage them to correct themselves and to demand more elaborate forms of speech. In such situations it is important not to discourage students, but to provide them with another attainable goal.

On the other hand, there are students who study English mainly in the class. They tend to be shy about speaking a foreign language and there are a few problems which make it almost impossible for them to utter a word. First of all, speaking is done under the pressure of time. A student must respond relatively quickly and there is not much time to think or check something in the dictionary. Another issue connected with timing is that most students up to the intermediate level think in their mother tongues. So, to say anything they need time to translate into the target language. Learners often complain 'How can I talk about it? I wouldn't even know what to say in my language.' However, the next thing they realize is that word-for-word translation does not work in most cases. Therefore, teachers should facilitate oral tasks with models to follow. Another problem is that some students are so afraid of making mistakes that they refuse to speak completely. I think pair or group work could help solve this problem.

What did you learn about speaking on your own teacher-training course?
To tell the truth, I don't really remember what I actually learnt on my own teacher-training course. I won't be able to separate it from the knowledge I gained by self-studying or at methodological conferences. What I recall are methods of teaching a foreign language, out of which the audiolingual and communicative approaches are probably still the most popular in teaching speaking. I also remember the time creating devices, which are when the speaker is given time to think about what to say next. We looked at different techniques for correcting mistakes in oral production as well as ideas about what kind of tasks to use. I also remember being told that speaking is facilitated by listening.

Have you applied what you learnt on your training course to your own classes?
It was natural for me to apply the knowledge I acquired as well as my own experience with learning a foreign language to my own classes. Of course I quite liked using the audiolingual method with all kinds of drills because I used this technique when I learnt. It turned out to be effective but boring over a longer period. I am still enchanted with the communicative approach as it gives the sense of achievement very quickly. But what I realized about teaching and learning methods in general, which is probably true not only for speaking, is that the process can't be boring.

How do you help students who have problems with speaking?
The most effective way to teach students speaking is to encourage them to speak the language a lot. So to help them I give a lot of various speaking tasks, which I always try to facilitate with a list of useful expressions and vocabulary. I often give them a model to imitate. To help overcome shyness I ask my students to work in pairs and mixed groups and then ask them to report to the whole class, starting with the more fluent ones and finishing with the weaker ones. I am very careful to pick interesting topics for discussions. To ensure that they listen to each other I sometimes introduce a kind of game, Suspense, for example, 'Listen to your friend's three stories and ask him/her some questions to find out which of the stories is a lie.' And perhaps the most important thing about teaching speaking is that I show interest in what my students want to tell me.

How do you integrate speaking with the teaching of other skills?
Speaking is, in my opinion, the easiest skill to integrate with the other skills. Almost every lesson starts with a speaking task as a way of introducing new vocabulary, eliciting what the students already know about the subject,

getting their attention, making them think about the new topic. Now with the new form of school-leaving exam, Polish teachers use more picture descriptions both as an introductory or a key element of the lesson. Speaking also serves as an excellent follow-up activity. It may be a discussion after reading a text or doing a listening, or as supplementary activity for a grammar exercise.

Finally, I'd like to say that working with young people is a very demanding task because they tend to rebel against everything, but at the same time it is one of the most rewarding jobs as they react very spontaneously and if you try, you can achieve a lot together.

QUESTIONS

1　What does Małgorzata think are the main problems for students who speak English outside the classroom?

　A　They worry about making mistakes.
　B　They don't use complex forms of speech and don't correct themselves.
　C　They aren't confident about speaking English.

2　What does Małgorzata think are the main problems for students who usually speak English in the classroom?

　A　They are very confident about speaking and make a lot of mistakes.
　B　They always think in English.
　C　They are under time pressures and are nervous of making mistakes.

3　Complete the sentence below with the most suitable option.

　　On her teacher-training course Małgorzata learnt that practice in … is very helpful in teaching speaking.

　A　writing
　B　listening
　C　reading

4　Małgorzata thinks that the audiolingual method:

　A　works well but can be boring
　B　doesn't work well
　C　works well and the students like it

5　In Małgorzata's opinion working in pairs and groups helps students:

　A　overcome shyness
　B　make fewer mistakes
　C　get more speaking practice

6　In Małgorzata's opinion the most important thing in teaching speaking is to:

　A　show an interest in what the students are saying
　B　make sure that all errors are corrected

c make sure students speak to each other

7   Tick the speaking activities that Małgorzata mentions which are often used at
the beginning of a lesson:

a introducing new vocabulary   ☐
b giving instructions for the lesson   ☐
c talking about the weekend   ☐
d eliciting what students already know about a subject   ☐
e correcting homework   ☐
f   getting students' attention   ☐
g making them think about the new topic   ☐

8   Which of the following does Małgorzata NOT mention as a follow-up speaking
activity?

A   a discussion after reading or hearing a text
B   a supplementary activity for a grammar exercise
c   checking answers

ACTIVITY

Read through Małgorzata's account of her teaching experience and practice.
Which of the interactive activities listed on pages 65 to 67 does she mention using
with her classes?

Chapter 6
Reading HANA ŠVECOVÁ

Hana Švecová is a teacher, teacher trainer, and author. She has extensive
experience teaching and training in the Czech Republic.

*What in your view are the major problems for your students when learning to
read in a foreign language?*
Reading exposes learners to vocabulary and language they are not familiar
with. My students often worry about failing to understand everything and
try to use the dictionary. Looking up all the unknown words from the text is
very slow and boring. They often need a lot of time just to get past a few
sentences. Sometimes even the dictionary does not help. My students
sometimes tell me that they do understand the meaning of all the individual
words in the sentence, but the overall meaning is still unclear. It discourages
them from further reading because they feel the effort invested is not worth
the outcome.

What did you learn about reading on your own teacher-training course?
I learnt that it was important to structure a reading task not to overwhelm
learners by unknown language, but help them focus on what is important

and make the task look 'doable'. Sometimes even pre-teaching a few words can do the trick. I found out that it was not always effective to read and understand everything in detail, but using strategies such as skimming or scanning can be more productive.

Have you applied what you learnt on your training course to your own classes?
I often use scanning and skimming with my students in class. I have found out that if they focus on looking for a specific piece of information or reading a passage very quickly, they actually worry less about not understanding everything. I try to make clear that I do not expect them to study the text in detail, but want them to do a particular task. I think it is useful to introduce reading by, for example, asking learners what they know about the topic, doing a pre-reading task from the coursebook, or pre-teaching some key words from the text.

How do you help students who have problems with reading?
If students want to improve their reading skills, it is important for them to stay in regular contact with the language. This is often a problem because reading is rarely seen as an enjoyable activity. I am enthusiastic about using graded readers for introducing more reading. Readers work with a limited range of vocabulary and language, and that is why learners can follow the story in the book and understand 'everything' without using the dictionary. Such reading often gives learners a sense of achievement, which can motivate further reading.

Sometimes it is also useful to look for a link between reading skills learners have already built in their first language and reading in the foreign language.

How do you integrate reading with the teaching of other skills?
I think learners do much more reading during the lesson than we sometimes realize. It is often the type of reading that has been integrated with other skills. For example, they often need to read instructions before they start doing a speaking or listening exercise, or they make notes and then need to read them to be able to report back. I also think there is a natural partnership between reading and writing. All stages of editing a text actually include reading.

QUESTIONS

1 Hana thinks learners can be discouraged from reading because:

   A they think they have to work very hard to understand every word
   B there are too many unknown words in the texts they read
   C they only read a few sentences

2 On her teacher-training course Hana learnt that:

   A learners need to understand every word of a text
   B a pre-reading activity is always useful
   C learners need to study a text in detail in order to understand it

3   Complete the sentence below with the most appropriate option:

Structured activities can help learners ...

A focus on what is important in a text
B understand a text in detail
C understand all the words in a text

4   Are the following statements true or false according to Hana?

A If learners read a passage quickly, they worry less about understanding every word.
B It isn't helpful to ask learners to focus on a particular piece of information in a text.
C A pre-reading activity can teach learners some of the words they don't know before they read a text.

5   Which of the following pre-reading activities does Hana NOT mention?

A pre-teaching some important words from the text
B asking learners what they know about the topic in the text
C getting learners to write some questions they want to find the answers to

6   Graded readers are:

A books which tell a story
B books which use a restricted range of vocabulary and language
C books which help learners use a dictionary

7   Hana thinks that students do more reading than we realize because:

A reading is often integrated with the other skills
B students read a lot at home
C reading is an enjoyable activity

8   Which of the skills does Hana think forms a natural combination with reading?

A speaking
B listening
C writing

ACTIVITY

Read through Hana's account of her teaching experience and practice. In what ways does she get her students to practise the various reading skills listed on page 70?

Chapter 7
Writing MELISSA LAMB

Melissa Lamb has been a teacher for nine years. She worked in China for five years and now teaches at International House in London.

What in your view are the major problems for students when learning to write in a foreign language?
I think writing is one of the skills which is most overlooked in EFL lessons. It's one of the skills that both students and teachers are scared of and a skill that everyone finds difficult for a variety of reasons. Mainly because when you write something it is deemed important, it's ever-lasting and permanent and so therefore a lot of importance is placed on the final text.

The major problems students have therefore are psychological, but there are also problems in terms how we construct what we write. Before they write, getting ideas is often a huge problem for students, and while they are writing, simple things like organization, style, register, coherence, cohesion of the text create all sorts of barriers for students if they don't know how to put text together. And then of course there are the obvious issues of grammar and vocabulary in terms of both range and accuracy. So, writing can seem like an insurmountable challenge to students and, of course, it involves so many different aspects and sub-skills it can seem a very difficult area to focus on for a teacher as well.

What sort of things do you think teachers can do to help learners with writing?
In the last couple of years I have taught a lot of exam classes which involve a lot of writing. In both IELTS and the Cambridge exams students have to try to attempt to do a wide range of writing tasks. In the past few months I have come to the conclusion that confidence building and getting students interested in writing are both crucial, and that before any writing occurs, it is vital to create ideas. I have found that my students' work has been a lot better since they have spent at least fifty per cent of the class time doing mind maps, vocabulary-building, and sharing information and ideas. I also use texts a lot with my students to give them models for writing. So we analyse texts as a starting point and look at the component parts like the overall organization, the style, and the register.

Do you think it is easy for teachers to integrate writing with the other skills?
I think teachers combine writing with a lot of other skills even though sometimes they don't know they are doing it. So, for example they do dictation activities, or various spelling and punctuation activities. A lot of listening activities also use writing. For example, a listening text can be used to practise note-taking skills, or there are a number of while-listening activities in which students need to write, even if it is just filling in a gap. These can help students focus on accuracy in terms of word formation or spelling. Both reading and listening texts are incredibly useful for giving a context for any writing activity and providing students with an opportunity to hear or read the kind of language they are expected to produce.

I also combine writing with drawing so, for example, the students might have to draw something and then label it and then expand those notes into sentences. With lower levels, students can practise writing dialogues or role-plays. These activities are very good for giving students the confidence to then stand up and do the role-play, particularly with elementary students. Students can also do a lot of less formal writing. For example, they can write a diary either for themselves or for the teacher.

Do you think teachers learn enough about teaching writing on their teacher-training courses?

I think teachers in general need to know more about writing and how to teach writing, and I think it's something that there should be more of on teacher-training courses. The most important thing to remember about any writing task is that it needs to be broken down into little sections so that students can build up the component parts which make a good piece of writing.

QUESTIONS

1 Melissa thinks students are nervous about writing because:

   A when you write you leave a permanent record
   B writing has to be properly organised
   C English spelling is very difficult

2 Tick the elements that Melissa mentions that students need to know about for writing:

   a spelling ☐
   b organization ☐
   c paragraphing ☐
   d register ☐
   e punctuation ☐
   f coherence ☐
   g grammar ☐
   h alphabet ☐

3 Complete the sentence below with the most appropriate phrase from the list.

   Before we start writing Melissa thinks it is important to create …

   A a structure
   B ideas
   C outline notes

4 Melissa uses texts as:

   A practice in listening
   B information on a topic
   C models for a written text

5 Melissa thinks gap-filling exercises can help students:

   A focus on register
   B focus on spelling and accuracy

c focus on expanding their vocabulary

6 Reading and listening texts can give students the chance to:

A hear or read some of the language they might need

B practise note-taking

c practise word formation

7 Which of the options below (A, B, C) completes the sequence (1, 2, 3) Melissa describes which begins with drawing?

1 students draw something

2 students label what they have drawn

3 ...

A students talk about what they have drawn

B students expand their notes into sentences

c students draw a second picture for the other students to label

8 Melissa thinks the most important element of teaching writing is to:

A break the task down into manageable sections

B give students informal writing practice

c get students to keep a diary

ACTIVITY

Read through Melissa's account of her teaching experience and practice. Which of the skills needed for writing which are listed on page 87 does Melissa concentrate on in her writing classes?

Chapter 8

Planning CATHERINE XIANG

Catherine Xiang is from Shanghai in China. She is currently doing a PhD at the Open University in the UK as well as teaching Chinese at the University of Bristol. Before that she was a language teacher in Shanghai where she taught both English and Mandarin Chinese to adults. She has also taught young learners.

How important do you think lesson planning is?
I think lesson planning is quite important but I also think how important planning is depends on the experience of the teacher and on whether the teacher is familiar with what he or she is doing. I think the whole reason for planning a lesson is to help yourself be clear about what you want to do and how you are going to do it. So I think planning is important as a way of providing guidance for yourself so that you know the focus of the class. But I don't think a plan needs to be very detailed. It is important to be able to

change the lesson plan and adjust what you do according to the needs of the students rather than just the lesson plan.

How much time do you spend planning your own lessons?
The length of time I spend planning a lesson depends. If I'm planning a brand new lesson that I have never taught before with students I don't know, I would probably spend much longer getting new material, getting myself familiarized with the text book, and thinking about the activities that I would like to use. Normally say for a 60-minute lesson I might take a similar sort of time to plan. The amount of time I spend also depends whether I have got enough teaching materials or if I need to create my own. Collecting materials, drawing pictures, and that sort of thing does take a long time. But I think the actual constructing and the thinking time might be equivalent to the lesson.

What are the main things you consider when you are planning a lesson?
The first thing I would want to think about in planning a lesson is how much time I have. In planning a lesson you need to decide how much time you are going to spend reviewing things, and how much time you are actually going to spend on new stuff. I think dividing up the time properly is very important. I also like to use a wide range of different activities and focus on different skills. With younger students in particular you have to have a lot of variety and think of different ways to get their attention all the time. So for example, first we'll do a grammar task and then maybe we'll sing a song and then maybe we will move to talking or a role-play or something similar. I note all these things and how much time I am going to spend on each in my plans.

Do you keep your lesson plans and do you need to revise them?
I keep my lesson plans for a short time but I nearly always change them or re-write them because I think with different students you always have to change something and you always have to be flexible about revising your plans. I have found that as I become more experienced and confident in class I need to make less detailed plans, and I am able to adapt things during the lesson.

QUESTIONS

1 Catherine thinks a lesson plan:

   A always needs to be very detailed
   B doesn't always need to be very detailed
   C doesn't matter at all

2 In Catherine's opinion it is important to:

   A keep to the exact details of your lesson plan
   B make sure the students know the details of your lesson plan
   C be able to change your plan according to the students' needs

3 For a new 60-minute lesson Catherine usually spends:

   A 60 minutes planning the lesson

   B 30 minutes planning the lesson

   C 120 minutes planning the lesson

4 Which of the following does NOT affect the amount of time needed to plan a lesson in Catherine's opinion?

   A whether she has the appropriate materials

   B whether she knows the students

   C whether the lesson focuses on skills or grammar

5 Complete the sentence below with the most appropriate phrase.

   Catherine thinks that … is the most important element of lesson planning.

   A knowing how you will divide the time

   B knowing how many students you have

   C knowing what level your students are at

6 Complete the sentence below with the most appropriate phrase.

   Catherine says that with younger learners it is essential to have a lot of … :

   A variety

   B songs

   C speaking activities

7 Which of these options does Catherine mention in her description of a lesson with young learners?

   A students practise writing

   B students practise speaking

   C students do a grammar task

   D students sing a song

8 Catherine constantly changes her lesson plans because:

   A she has become more confident in class

   B she would get bored of the plan if she used it more than once

   C she feels that different plans are needed for different students

ACTIVITY

Read through Catherine's account of her teaching experience and practice. How many of the elements needed for planning listed on page 103 does she mention in her account?

Chapter 9

Assessment YUKO KIKUCHI

Yuko Kikuchi is a primary English teacher in Japan.

Which national or international foreign language examinations have you taken?
I took the Japanese national test for English, the STEP (Society for Testing English Proficiency) Test, known in Japanese as 'Eiken'. At the lower levels this is mainly a written test with a listening comprehension at the end. Once a student has reached Grade 3, they have an interview test which is done one-on-one. The examinee is asked to read a text and is expected to answer questions from the examiner. At this level, learners are able to hold a simple conversation about matters of daily life – make and reply to greetings, introduce someone, make purchases, etc. They can read simple materials – letters, signboards, notices, etc., and write about themselves in elementary English.

I also took TOEIC which was challenging and gave me a feeling of achievement after I'd taken it.

Which examinations do you have to prepare your learners for?
TOEFL, Eiken, junior high school and high school exams, and/or university entrance exams.

How does this affect your teaching, for example, curriculum and lesson content?
It affects it a lot. I have to change my teaching style and materials completely.

Are there any exams that you feel are a good way of assessing your learners?
I am interested in the Cambridge Young Learners English (YLE) tests. There are three levels: Starters, Movers, and Flyers. I am now thinking of modifying my curriculum to meet the levels. It requires at least 100 to 120 hours of studying and it means that it will take three years after the children have started learning English – my children and I only meet once a week for 60 to 90 minutes.

Have you developed any ways of assessing the progress of your learners?
Yes, I use a chart that shows the 50 to 100 items that I teach the children. The items are things like telling the time, reading aloud from a picture book, saying the numbers one to twenty, and putting alphabet cards in order. Either they can check by themselves or I check and make a note if they can say certain things in English or answer questions their classmates or I ask. I try to make sure that assessing learners encourages them to continue learning and become more competent than they are now. Here is an example of what I mean. The chart is written in Japanese so that the children can read and choose the item. When a child is able to successfully do something I draw a smiley face on the card.

1	2	3
You can say your own telephone number ☺	You can say what time it is. ☺	You can say words that start with the letters v, s, z, h, m, n. ☺
4	**5**	**6**
You can read capital letters on well-shuffled cards.	You can say 'I'll have this one' when you choose something. ☺	You can say the months of the year from January to December. ☺

QUESTIONS

1 At grade 3 of the STEP examination the learners have an interview with:

   A one examiner
   B one other student
   C two examiners

2 At grade 3 of the STEP examination learners have to:

   A listen to a text and answer questions about it
   B read a text and answer questions about it
   C write a text and answer questions about it

3 Which of the following do learners NOT have to do for grade 3 of the STEP exam?

   A read simple letters
   B reply to greetings
   C write an essay

4 Yuko feels that:

   A she doesn't have to change her teaching style to fit in with examinations
   B she has to change her teaching style to fit in with examinations
   C examinations are not relevant to how we teach

5 The Cambridge Young Learners English tests require at least:

   A 50 to 100 hours of study
   B 60 to 90 hours of study
   C 100 to 120 hours of study

6 Yuko uses a chart to show the learners the:

   A mistakes that the learners make
   B things the learners can do
   C things the learners haven't learnt yet

7 Tick the items that Yuko mentions she puts on her chart:

  a telling the time   ☐
  b giving directions   ☐
  c alphabet   ☐
  d colours   ☐
  e reading aloud   ☐
  f saying numbers   ☐
  g describing a person ☐

8 Yuko feels it is important that assessment should:

  A encourage the learners to continue learning
  B be a thorough test of a learner's knowledge
  c help a learner to see what they have to focus on

ACTIVITY

Read through Yuko's account of her teaching experience and practice. How does she deal with any of the issues relating to testing which are listed on page 123?

CLASSROOM LANGUAGE

Learner–teacher interaction

LEARNER	TEACHER
What does [kleptomaniac] mean?	It's someone who wants to steal something.
How do you say [maison] in English?	'House.'
How do you spell [blanket]?	b-l-a-n-k-e-t
Could I have a pencil, please?	Certainly.
May I be excused?	Sure.
May I open the window?	OK.
I haven't got a partner.	Can you work in a three with Mario and Maria?
What should I do?	Open your book on page 49.
I've finished.	Well done. Can I see?

Learner–learner interaction

LEARNER 1	LEARNER 2
Whose turn is it?	Mine, I think.
	Yours, I think.
It's your turn.	OK.
Have we finished?	I think so.
Shall we do the next question?	Sure.
Do you mean …?	That's right.
	No, what I meant was …
Could you say that again?	Yeah. …
I'm sorry, I didn't catch that.	[repeats what they said]
What do you think?	I'm not sure but …
I think …	Really …

Teacher's instructions and explanations

Explaining an activity
In this activity we're going to …
You need to share the information you have to find a solution.
Find ten similarities/differences between your picture and your partner's.
I want you to imagine …

Today we are going to …
In this lesson/activity I want you to …
First of all I'd like you to …
Here's an example of …
Let me give/show you an example.

Organizing the class
I'd like you to work in pairs / groups of four.
Could you two work together?
You three get into a group.
Leo, can you work with Marie?
Has everyone got a partner?
Can you sit facing (away from) each other?
Can you stand back to back?
Everyone stand up / sit down.
Get into two teams.
Could you come to the front of the class?

Instructions and requests
Ask each other the questions you've prepared.
Make a note of your answers.
Ask your partner to tell you about …
[Paulo], you're going to be …
I'd like [Boris] to be the chairperson in this group. His job is to make sure
that everyone has a chance to speak.
Can I have your homework please?
Could someone clean the board, please?
Could you close the window, please?
Sit down, please.
Listen everyone.
Let's look at the first activity.
Can you read the first text, Henri?
Try after me [teacher models sentence]
Compare your answers with the person sitting next to you.

Eliciting
Is that right?
Kumiko, what's the answer for number …?
What do you think, Saard?
Could you say that again / repeat that?
What's this?
What have you got for number …?
Any ideas for number …?
Who knows the answer to number …?
What do you think about …?

Do you all agree on the answer?

Correction
Look at this sentence. Is there anything wrong with it?
How would you correct this sentence?
Try that sentence again using the past tense.
What word usually goes after 'traffic'?

LEARNER   I go to town yesterday.
TEACHER   I *went* to town yesterday.
LEARNER   I went to town yesterday.

LEARNER   I go to town yesterday.
TEACHER   I 'go' (?) to town yesterday.
LEARNER   I went to town yesterday.

LEARNER   I go to town yesterday.
TEACHER   What's the past of 'go'?
LEARNER   'Went'. I went to town yesterday.

Setting time limits
I'll give you ten minutes to do this.
You have ten minutes to do this.
Two more minutes.

Ending an activity
Let's finish now.
Time's up.
Could you all sit down, please?

Feedback
Very well done.
Excellent.
Good.
I think we need to do that again.

Checking instructions
Has everyone got that?
OK?
Does everyone understand?
Has anyone got any questions?
Julia, are you working with Ken or Mario?
Can you all hear that?

Social comments /small talk
Did you have a good weekend?
What did you do at the weekend?
What are you going to do this evening / this weekend?

Apologies
I'm sorry I'm late.
I'm afraid I haven't finished my homework.
I'm afraid I've lost my notebook.

GLOSSARY

This is a glossary of the items that appear in bold in the preceding chapters. The numbers in brackets [ ] refer to the page where the word appears for the first time.

accuracy the production of language which does not contain errors [13]

achievement test a test based on the work learners have done during a course. [122]

acquire to learn something in an informal or non-conscious way, for example, picking up a phrase and incorporating it into your vocabulary without being aware of actually doing so. [24]

active learner a learner who takes a positive approach to their learning. [2]

active listening a positive approach by learners to understand what is said to them and to have some control over the interactive process. [47]

(an) activity what the learners do in the classroom. This is usually organized and has an aim. [5]

aim what the teacher and learners plan to achieve. [1]

antonym a word that has the opposite meaning to another, for example, 'quick' and 'slow'. [30]

automating the use of language by learners without conscious processing. [12]

auxiliary verb a verb that is used with the main verb to perform a grammatical function such as forming a question, showing whether an action has finished, etc. [107]

brainstorm to generate as many ideas as possible around a single topic. [76]

closed pairs two learners work together without the class listening. [64]

closed question a question which limits the type of answer possible. [107]

coherence the linking of parts of a text so that the text makes sense. [87]

cohesion the integration of parts of a text. [87]

collocate the way in which certain words often occur together, for example, 'make the bed'. [33]

concept an idea behind the use of a particular form, for example, the concept of countability and the use or non-use of the plural 's' ('bananas', 'rice'). [115]

concept question a question to check whether learners have understood the meaning of a structure. [41]

connected speech spoken language in which individual words sometimes link up. [60]

consonants the letters of the alphabet excluding vowels, i.e. 'b', 'c', 'd', 'f', etc. [27]

context the background to and situation in which we hear, read, or use language. [2]

decode to break down what is said or written into its component parts in order to be able to comprehend it. [47]

diagnostic test tests which identify learners' specific strengths and weaknesses. [103]

dialogue an **exchange** between two people, for example, two people talking about a TV programme they have both seen. [18]

dictation an activity in which a text is read out loud and the learners write it down as accurately as possible. [17]

distractor the incorrect answer in a multiple-choice question. [126]

drill a controlled activity which gives spoken practice of target language through the teacher providing prompts which the learners give the appropriate response to. [17]

elicit asking learners to provide a response. The response could be part of an exchange ('Would you like to have lunch?' – I'd love to.'), provide information ('What's the capital of South Korea?' – 'Seoul.'), and so on. [83]

encode put a message together using the components of the language. [27]

ESP English for Specific Purposes. English which focuses on particular lexical or grammatical fields that learners will need in order to understand a particular subject, for example, medicine or dentistry. [114]

examination a procedure for measuring ability or knowledge usually at institutional level, for example, 'UCLES' (University of Cambridge Local Examinations Syndicate), which leads to a qualification. [121]

exchange communication between two or more people, for example, a conversation. [57]

exponent the way a **function** is expressed, for example, 'Would you like to...?' is an exponent for making an offer. [36]

extrinsic relating to external factors such as social pressure, or institutional requirements (examinations and qualifications). [7]

false start when a speaker starts to say something and then goes back and rephrases the beginning of the utterance. [47]

filler words and noises such as 'Well', 'Um', or 'I mean', which speakers use to give themselves time to think about what they are saying. [60]

fluency producing spoken language without unnecessary pauses, false starts, or repetition. [12]

form the way a regular pattern of language is represented in spoken or written English, for example, the form of the present perfect is 'have' or 'has' + past participle. [18]

(the) four skills speaking, listening, reading, and writing. [2]

function what we do with language, for example, apologize, explain. [20]

gap fill a text in which individual words are missing. [94]

gist the general ideas in a text. [46]

grading the order in which things can be taught, from the simplest to the more complex. [115]

group work a practice activity involving three or more learners. [20]

handouts items which are given to learners at the beginning of an activity, for example, a **worksheet**. [103]

homophone words which are spelt differently but sound the same, for example, 'see' and 'sea'. [28]

immersion using the target language all the time in your daily life. [8]

information gap when one person has information that another person doesn't have. [24]

input all the target language that a learner is aware of, either spoken or written. [11]

interact communicate with two or more people. [27]

interaction patterns the ways in which learners and teacher communicate with each other, for example, pairs, groups, whole class. [105]

intonation the change in pitch of the voice when someone speaks. [31]

intransitive (verb) a verb which does not take an object. [31]

intrinsic relating to internal factors such as wishes and desires. [7]

L1 a learner's first language. [2]

L2 a learner's second language, i.e. the language they are studying. [23]

lexis another word for **vocabulary**. [116]

linking joining words together when they are spoken. [30]

long-term memory where we store language and information. [71]

meaning language has meaning when it refers to a person, thing, or concept that can be understood by other speakers of the same language. [1]

message the content of what someone says or writes. [12]

method the way we do something. 'Method' with a capital 'M' refers to a broader set of beliefs about languages and how they should be taught. [15]

modal verb an **auxiliary verb** which indicates the attitude of the speaker, for example, 'You *should* take it easy'. [107]

monitor check the learners' use of the language. [65]

motivation a reason or set of reasons to do something. This can be **intrinsic** or **extrinsic**. [7]

needs analysis a survey or study which finds out what the learners need to learn. [114]

noticing a term for learners focussing their attention on an item of language in order to understand it and use it. [11]

noun phrase a group of words based around a noun, for example, 'bus stop', 'the bus stop where I met my first girlfriend'. [27]

open pair two learners speak while the class listen. [5]

open question a question that does not require a particular answer and can be of any length. [106]

oral an adjective referring to speaking. [20]

pair work an activity involving two learners practising a particular skill or a language item. [20]

paralinguistic features features of communication which do not involve speech, for example, gestures or facial expressions. [48]

part of speech a grammatical category of a word, for example, 'clean' is an adjective, 'run' is a verb. [31]

passive listening when you listen to something without responding or taking control of the listening process in any way. [47]

pattern a group of words that often occur together. [11]

phoneme the individual sounds in a language. [27]

phonetic chart a chart that shows how letters are pronounced. [29]

phonetic language a language in which the spelling and the sound are the same. English is not a phonetic language. [28]

portfolio a collection of a learner's work used to evaluate the learner's progress. [130]

post-listening activity an activity that learners do after listening to something. [49]

PPP Presentation–Practice–Production [20]

prefix an element that can be added to the beginning of a word to change its meaning, for example, 'happy' – '**un**happy'. [32]

pre-listening activity an activity that prepares learners for a listening text. [49]

progress test a test given during a course to see how far a learner's language ability has developed [121]

prompt what a teacher says to elicit a response from a learner. [63]

pronunciation the way a sound or combination of sounds is produced. [30]

reader a book which has been simplified for language learners. [69]

realia real objects such as packaging, magazines, leaves, stamps, etc. [104]

recycle to revise things previously studied and relate them to what is being currently studied. [114]

register variation in the style in which a person speaks or writes depending on the situation. [69]

role play an activity in which learners take on different parts and act out a situation. [20]

scaffolding providing carefully structured support for learning. [4]

schwa the phonetic symbol /ə/ used to show an unstressed vowel. [54]

stress where the emphasis is placed on a word or sentence when speaking, for example, the first syllable of 'telephone' is stressed – /'teləfeʊn/. An example of sentence stress is 'I **love** you' as opposed to 'I love **you**.' [29]

structure a relatively fixed pattern of language which can be adapted to fit a context, for example, 'if' + present simple + 'will' to talk about the possible future, 'If it rains tomorrow, I'll stay at home.' [16]

suffix what can be added to the end of a word to change its function, for example, 'happy' – 'happily'. [32]

syllable a unit of speech which can be made up of a single vowel, for example, 'a', or a combination of vowels and consonants, for example, 'bough'. [29]

synonym a word that has a similar meaning to another, for example, 'quick' and 'fast'. [30]

target language the language system that learners are aiming to learn, for example, for Japanese learners of English, English is the target language. [8]

task an activity which has a purpose (other than that of using the target language) and an outcome, for example, doing a class survey of leisure activities to find out the most popular pastime. [17]

test a procedure for evaluating knowledge and ability. [121]

text an example of the **target language**. These can be spoken texts – conversations, speeches, quotes, and so on; or written texts – a newspaper article, a short story, a novel, a report, a composition, etc. [2]

time line a visual representation of how time is referred to using the present and past tenses, 'going to', the present perfect, etc. [39]

transitive (verb) a verb which takes an object. [31]

turn one speaker's part in an **exchange**. [58]

unstressed where there is no emphasis on a spoken word or sentence, for example, the second syllable of 'telephone' is not stressed – /'teləfeʊn/. [29]

utterance what someone says. This may be a series of sentences, a single sentence, a clause, phrase, or word. [58]

verb phrase a group of words based around a verb, for example, 'get', 'get on', 'get on with', 'get on with the other learners in the class'. [27]

vocabulary all the words in a particular language. [2]

vowel 'a', 'e', 'i', 'o', 'u' The English alphabet is made up of five vowels and twenty **consonants**. There are 44 sounds. [27]

working memory the part of the memory we use to hold information and language for a short time. [71]

worksheet a paper handout which contains an activity, task, or exercise. [103]

FURTHER READING

This is a list of books that provide more information and teaching ideas relating to the nine topics in the book.

1 Learning and teaching English

Lightbown, P. and **N. Spada.** 2006. *How Languages are Learned, 3rd Edition.* Oxford: Oxford University Press.

Brown, H. 1994. *Principles of Language Learning and Teaching.* Englewood Cliffs, New Jersey: Prentice Hall Regents.

Harmer, J. 2001. *The Practice of English Language Teaching.* London: Longman.

Hedge, T. 2000. *Teaching and Learning in the Language Classroom.* Oxford: Oxford University Press.

2 Teaching methods and ideas

Larsen-Freeman, D. 2000. *Teaching Techniques in English as a Second Language.* Oxford: Oxford University Press.

Richards, J. and **T. Rogers.** 1986. *Approaches and Methods in Language Teaching* Cambridge: Cambridge University Press.

Howatt, A. P. R. 2004. *A History of English Language Teaching, 2nd Edition.* Oxford: Oxford University Press.

The coursebook examples come from:

Hornby, A. S. and **R. Mackin.** 1964. *Oxford Progressive English Alternative Course Book A.* Oxford: Oxford University Press. (out of print)

Hartley, B. and **P. Viney.** 1978. *Streamline Departures Teacher's Edition.* Oxford: Oxford University Press.

Soars, L. and **J.** 2000. *New Headway English Course Elementary Student's Book.* Oxford: Oxford University Press.

Oxenden, C., C. Latham-Koenig, and **P. Seligson.** 2005. *New English File Pre-intermediate Student's Book.* Oxford: Oxford University Press.

Whitney, N. 1994. *Open Doors 1 Student's Book.* Oxford: Oxford University Press.

3 Language

Hadfield, J. and C. 1999. *Oxford Basics: Presenting New Language*. Oxford: Oxford University Press.

Scrivener, J. 2003. *Oxford Basics: Teaching Grammar*. Oxford: Oxford University Press.

Swan, M. 2001. *The Good Grammar Book*. Oxford: Oxford University Press.

Swan, M. 2005. *Practical English Usage, 3rd Edition*. Oxford: Oxford University Press.

Ur, Penny. 1988 *Grammar Practice Activities*. Cambridge: Cambridge University Press.

4 Listening

Hadfield, J. and C. 1999. *Oxford Basics: Simple Listening Activities*. Oxford: Oxford University Press.

Švecová, H. 2006. *Listen and Do*, Oxford: Oxford University Press.

White, G. 1998. *Resource Books for Teachers: Listening*. Oxford: Oxford University Press.

Ur, P. 1984. *Teaching Listening Comprehension*. Cambridge: Cambridge University Press.

5 Speaking

Hadfield, J. and C. 1999. *Oxford Basics: Simple Speaking Activities*. Oxford: Oxford University Press.

Kenworthy, J. 1987. *Teaching English Pronunciation*. London: Longman.

Klippel, F. 1985. *Keep Talking*. Cambridge: Cambridge University Press.

6 Reading

Hadfield, J. and C. 1999. *Oxford Basics: Simple Reading Activities*. Oxford: Oxford University Press.

Nuttall, C. 1982. *Teaching Reading Skills in A Foreign Language*. London: Heinemann.

Graded readers:

Let's Go Readers (Oxford University Press)
Dominoes (Oxford University Press)
Oxford Bookworms Library (Oxford University Press)

7 *Writing*

Reilly, J. and **V.** 2005. *Primary Resource Books for Teachers: Writing with Children.* Oxford: Oxford University Press.

Hadfield, J. and **C.** 1999. *Oxford Basics: Simple Writing Activities.* Oxford: Oxford University Press.

Hedge, T. 2005. *Resource Books for Teachers: Writing.* Oxford: Oxford University Press.

Wright, A. 1997. *Primary Resource Books for Teachers: Creating Stories with Children.* Oxford: Oxford University Press.

Barnard, R. and **A. Meehan.** 2005. *Writing for the Real World 2.* Oxford: Oxford University Press.

8 *Planning*

Nunan, D. 1988. *Syllabus Design.* Oxford: Oxford University Press.

Westrup, H. and **J. Baker.** 2004. *Oxford Basics: Activities Using Resources.* Oxford: Oxford University Press.

White, R. 1988. *The ELT Curriculum.* Oxford: Blackwell.

Woodward, T. 2001. *Planning Lessons and Courses.* Cambridge: Cambridge University Press.

9 *Assessment and evaluation*

Ioannou-Georgiou, S. and **P. Pavlou.** 2003. *Assessing Young Learners.* Oxford: Oxford University Press.

Heaton, J. 1991. *Writing English Language Tests.* London: Longman.

Hughes, A. 1989. *Testing for Language Teachers.* Cambridge: Cambridge University Press.

ANSWER KEY

Chapter 1   Learning and teaching English

ACTIVITY 2

These are the most likely meanings of the words from the text. Other answers are possible.

blaggar	coat or some other item of clothing
cofty	a drink of some kind
homeyshoes	comfortable house shoes, slippers
bestingest	favourite
fuff	sigh
dirky	difficult, tiring.

ACTIVITY 3

1 True   3 It depends   5 It depends
2 True   4 It depends   6 False

ACTIVITY 6

Could I have that thing you use to make pastry flat? [rolling pin]
Fancy a drink? – I would be delighted to accept your kind offer of a liquid refreshment.

Chapter 2   Teaching methods and ideas

ACTIVITY 3

1   Meeting someone for the first time – Young beginners
    The language here could include:
    Greetings – 'Hello. My name is ... What's yours?'
    Simple questions – 'Where are you from?' 'Where do you go to school?' 'What do you like doing in your spare time?' 'What's your favourite subject at school'? 'Do you have brothers and sisters?' 'Do you have any pets?'

2 Planning a night out with friends – Teenage intermediate learners
The language here could include:
Making suggestions – 'Let's …', 'Shall we…?' 'Why don't we …?' 'What about …?'
Making arrangements – 'What time / Where shall we meet?'

ACTIVITY 4

Possible solutions include:
1 Learners are shy about working in pairs or groups.
Model the activity yourself with a less shy learner first so everyone knows what they are doing. Move around the classroom encouraging everyone to speak.
2 The class is very large and the seats and desks cannot be moved.
Get the learners to turn round in their seats or sit on their desks facing backwards to work in small groups with the learners sitting behind them.
3 The class has to prepare for written, not spoken, exams.
When planning speaking activities, consider how these might be linked to written ones, for example, a role play about an interview for a college place could be linked to writing an application letter to the college.
4 Learners often ask for new vocabulary in English which you are unprepared for.
Teach your students to use a dictionary themselves – a very useful skill for them to have.

Chapter 3 Language

ACTIVITY 2

classroom	/klɑːsruːm/
desk	/desk/
student	/stjuːdnt/
listen	/lɪsn/
blackboard	/blækbɔːd/
pencil	/pensl/
teacher	/tiːtʃə/
book	/bʊk/

ACTIVITY 3

cla<u>ss</u>room	te<u>le</u>phone	im<u>por</u>tant	com<u>pu</u>ter	exa<u>m</u>ple
in<u>struc</u>tions	<u>ex</u>ercise	conver<u>sa</u>tion	ex<u>plain</u>	

ACTIVITY 4

Who loves me?	**I** love you.
What do you feel about me?	**I love** you.
Who do you love?	I love **you**.

ACTIVITY 5

Verb	Noun	Adjective	Opposite of adjective
employ	employment	employed	unemployed
believe	belief	believable	unbelievable
–	happiness	happy	unhappy
–	possibility	possible	impossible
educate	education	educated	uneducated
direct	direction	direct	indirect
comfort	comfort	comfortable	uncomfortable

ACTIVITY 6

Grammatical structure	Sample sentence	Function
Present continuous	He is writing a letter at the moment.	talk about a present activity
Present simple of 'to be'	My name is Mario.	state a fact
Past simple of 'to be'	His teacher was very strict.	state a fact about the past
Infinitive	Please put the book on the table.	give an instruction
Present perfect	I have cleaned the blackboard.	talk about a recent action
Past perfect	When I saw him he had grown a beard.	talk about an event which took place before another event in the past

ACTIVITY 7

get out of the way	Type B
she is going out with him	Type B
throw the rubbish away	Type A
take your shoes off	Type A

ACTIVITY 8

The train which has just arrived at platform one is out of service. [2]
Unless there is a shop in the village where they live, people who live in the countryside have to take the bus or drive to a supermarket to do their shopping. [4]

ACTIVITY 9

Expression	Function
Do you know what I mean?	checking that someone understands us (interactional)
Could you pass me that book?	asking someone to do something
What do you think?	asking for other people's opinions
I'm not sure I agree.	disagreeing
Can I just say …?	interrupting
I'm really sorry.	apologizing
Do you mean…?	checking that we have understood someone (interactional)
I don't think it should be allowed.	expressing our opinions
You can switch it on here.	giving instructions/information
Sorry, I didn't catch that.	asking for repetition (interactional)

ACTIVITY 10

A Hello, Bangor 35363.
B Oh hello, can I speak to Martin, please?
A I'm sorry, but he's not in at the moment
B Oh, OK. Do you know when he will be back?
A I'm not sure, but I think he has a meeting at two o'clock so he'll be back before then.
B I'm afraid I have to go out at that time. Will you tell him I called?
A Certainly. Could I have your name?
B It's John Jonson. He should have my number.
A Sorry, I didn't catch your surname. John …?
B The surname's Jonson.
A Is that J-O-H-N-S-O-N?
B It's actually without the 'h'.
A So that's J-O-N. Fine. I'll tell him you rang.
B Thank you. Goodbye.
A Goodbye.

ACTIVITY 11

Here are two example answers:

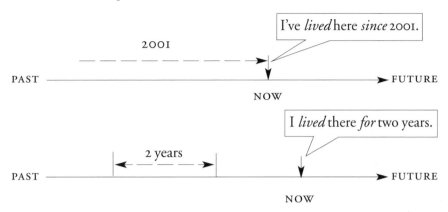

ACTIVITY 12

For ball sports we use 'play', for outdoor sports and activities 'go', and for indoor sports 'do'. One possibility is to show the learners pictures of the activities, making sure that a ball is visible in all the sports we 'play' and that it is clear that the outdoor activities are taking place outside. The pictures can be passed around the class and the learners given the task of writing the name of the activities and putting them into three groups according to the type of activities they are. To help, the teacher can ask guiding questions, for example, 'Do we use a ball to play tennis?' 'Do we go hiking inside?', and so on.

ACTIVITY 13

A Hi. How are you?
B Fine. And you? How was your weekend?
A Great. On Saturday I met some friends in town – we played tennis in the morning and went shopping in the afternoon.
B Sounds fun.
A It was great. How about you?
B I went walking on Saturday and did karate on Sunday. So I'm exhausted!

Here is one option:

Tell the class they are going to listen to two people talking about what they did last weekend. Give them a handout with gaps in the parts of the text where the question and answer forms occur:

1 How _____ your weekend?
2 I _____ some friends.
3 We _____ tennis.

4 How ____ ____ ?
5 I ____ walking.
6 I ____ karate.

The class listen to the conversation and fill in the gaps. They then work in pairs and ask and answer the same questions as the text.

Chapter 4 Listening

ACTIVITY 2

In a number of these situations it depends on the context whether you listen for gist or detail, but generally speaking:
– what someone says during a conversation: this depends on the conversation, but usually you will be listening for the general idea or 'normally'.
– announcements giving information: specific details
– the weather forecast on the radio: specific details
– a play on the radio: general idea / normally
– music: normally
– someone else's conversation (eavesdropping): general idea
– a lecture: this depends, but you are probably listening for specific details
– professional advice: specific details
– instructions: specific details
– directions: specific details
– a taped dialogue in class: this depends what you have been asked to do as you listen. If you are answering specific questions you will be listening for detail; if you are asked a general question you could be listening for gist; if you are asked just to listen you are probably listening 'normally'.

ACTIVITY 3

With many of these activities it will again depend on the actual situation in which you are listening. For example, normally a telephone conversation is active and you have to respond and interact with the other speaker, but if you are listening to a recorded message (for example, telling you about what's on at the cinema, or the opening hours of a tourist attraction) you obviously do not respond.
– what someone says during a conversation: active listening
– announcements giving information: passive listening
– the weather forecast on the radio: passive listening
– a play on the radio: passive listening
– music: passive listening
– someone else's conversation (eavesdropping): passive listening
– a lecture: passive listening

- professional advice: this depends; you could be active in this conversation for example, if you need to ask for clarification
- instructions: this depends; you could be active in this conversation too for example, if you need to ask for clarification.
- directions: as above
- dialogue in class: again this depends on what you are asked to do, but probably passive.

ACTIVITY 4

a – 4, b – 3, c – 2, d – 1, e – 5

ACTIVITY 5

a – complete a family tree; identify members of the family from a selection of pictures.
b – complete a form with incomplete information about what facilities are available; tick available facilities from a list.
c – tick from a list of statements about the environment which ones you hear; put the statements the speaker makes in order.
d – decide whether a list of statements about British schools are true or false; complete sentences about British schools; complete a chart showing the different stages of British schools.
e – decide which are the bad and good aspects of the speaker's job; complete a timetable of a normal day at work for the speaker.

ACTIVITY 6

Connected sounds are underlined. Unstressed vowels are in bold.
A Do you want me to make the dinner?
B That'd be nice.
A OK. What have we got in the fridge?
B Not a lot really. There isn't any meat. But I've got some pasta, and there are some tomatoes in the cupboard. And there's some cheese in the fridge.
A Right. That'll do. I can make some fresh tomato sauce for the pasta.

Chapter 5 Speaking

ACTIVITY 2

Speaker B makes the following sounds and words:
A Do you fancy going to the cinema tonight?
B Mmm [unenthusiastic]
A We could see that new romantic comedy.
B Oh I don't know [unenthusiastic]

A Or would you rather go out for a bite to eat?
B Oh [more enthusiastic]
A We could try that new Indian restaurant.
B Well [unenthusiastic]
A Or would you prefer Chinese?
B Yes – much better idea. [enthusiastic]

ACTIVITY 3

Speaking	Writing
Not usually planned or prepared beforehand.	1 Planned.
2 Speakers use incomplete or ungrammatical sentences. They can hesitate, repeat themselves, use fillers, for example, 'er … you know … well …'	Sentences are carefully organized and accurate.
Stress, intonation, gestures, and facial expressions carry meaning.	3 The meaning in a written text is not supported by other means except perhaps typography and surrounding images, as in an advert.
4 You can go back when speaking – points can be revised, repeated, and clarified at any time.	Writing is linear, i.e. it goes in one direction without repetitions or revisions.

ACTIVITY 4

The speaker uses the following fillers:
– Er   – You know   – Kind of   – The fact is …
– What I mean is…   – Sort of   – How shall I put it?   – I mean …

When I started to learn *er* German I found it *you know* quite easy. *What I mean is*, the vocabulary is very similar to *sort of* English, and the pronunciation is *how shall I put it* not hard. But then *the thing is* when you start to study the *kind of* grammar it gets much more *er* difficult. *The fact is*, I wish I had learnt it at school, *I mean* because the teachers made you *you know* do your homework and learn things by heart. Now, *the thing is* I just don't have the discipline.

ACTIVITY 5

One advantage of correcting at the end of an activity is that it avoids breaking the flow of communication and the risk of demotivating the learners. It also allows the learners to concentrate on the form of the language, ask the teacher questions, and consolidate their understanding. One disadvantage is that they have lost the opportunity to use the language correctly during the activity and may have reinforced the error. Some learners may prefer to be corrected when they make the mistake to avoid this perceived waste.

Chapter 6 Reading

ACTIVITY 2

'I'll have a coffee', 'I'd like a coffee.' or similar.

ACTIVITY 3

1   130 stories
2   Yes
3   The catalogue

In all three cases the reader needs to scan across the page, in a way that is very particular to websites. The headings and information are spread around the page in a very different way from books or newspapers. As the texts are very short the reader needs to briefly skim the text to find the relevant word or words.

ACTIVITY 4

Here are some possible answers:

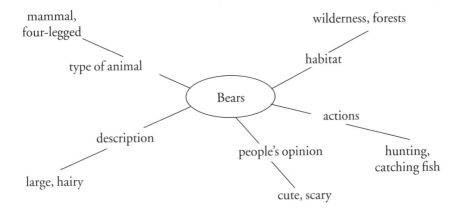

ACTIVITY 5

1   an autobiography; identify the text type
2   f, d, e, g-b-c, a; understand the sequence of events.
3   She spent a lot of time with him, played games with him; understand implications in the text

4 'we enjoyed ourselves *as much as we could*'; understand implications in the text

5 **we** – the writer and his mother, **there** – Rome, **that** – calling his mother; understand the word relationships within and between sentences.

6 'happy'; infer the meaning of a word

Chapter 7 Writing

ACTIVITY 2

More than one million people have begun to evacuate the Gulf Coast of the United States ahead of Hurricane Rita.

The writer expands the basic sentence by qualifying the number ('more than one million'); by specifying the time scale ('have begun...); and by specifying the time ('ahead of Hurricane Rita').

ACTIVITY 3

The pronouns in bold replace the nouns, which helps to avoid repetition:

John is a journalist. **He** went to London to meet Angela. **She** is **his** girlfriend. **He** met **her** at the station. **They** went to a restaurant and had lunch.

ACTIVITY 4

Dorna lived in London, where she went to school. She liked her school, but her parents moved to Manchester, where her mother found a job. Dorna went to a new school and made lots of new friends. Then she found a boyfriend who went to the same school. Dorna got very good grades in her exams but her boyfriend failed all his. She decided not to go to university because she wanted to stay with her boyfriend.

ACTIVITY 5

One way is to write down example sentences. Some structures can also be broken down into their individual elements and recorded, for example: the present perfect, 'I've lived here for three years'; 'have' + 'ed' + 'for' + time period.

ACTIVITY 7

sp   spelling
wo   word order
ww   wrong word
st   structure

t   tense
p   punctuation
rp re-phrase
\# number / concord (for example, verb-noun agreement)

ACTIVITY 8

sp   <u>Dere</u> Martin
p   I hope you are well/I am well.
p t   I am came to see you yesterday. <u>But</u> you <u>are</u> out. Please <u>to</u> telephone   st st
      <u>to</u> me
st ww when you can. I <u>will</u> have a party <u>in</u> <u>wednesday</u> and I <u>want that you</u>   p st
      <u>come</u>.
ww \# There will be <u>much funs</u> at the party.
wo   I <u>hope really</u> you can come.
      Maurizio

Chapter 8 Planning

ACTIVITY I

Other resources include:
– overhead projector: this can be useful for displaying the results of group work; you can cover or uncover sections of a transparency, for example, to tell a story, or to show correct answers.
– dictionaries (bilingual and monolingual): these can be useful for general practice in using a dictionary; also for collocations and pronunciation work.
– puppets: puppets (models of people or animals) can be useful for teaching younger learners. For example, dialogues can be acted out by two puppets, or you can have a puppet who only understands English to remind the children to use English.
– computers: CD-ROM or other software; internet and online resources. These can be useful for all sorts of activities. You can set up genuine communication activities if learners can communicate to each other or other people via email, for example. There are many online resources for language practice at all levels.

ACTIVITY 3

You would probably stand at the front of the class if you were explaining or demonstrating new language.

Standing at the back of the class enables the learners to carry out group work without feeling they are being constantly monitored and can help them feel more relaxed.

If you wanted to monitor pair or group work, you would move around the classroom and listen.

ACTIVITY 4

1 'What's this – anyone?' – This leaves the question open to anyone. The risk with this is that no-one will answer!
2 'What's this – Maria?' – This focuses on one learner. The risk here is that she won't know the answer. Springing the question on someone in this way makes sure that the learners pay attention in case they are asked. It also means the rest of the class might switch off for that question.
3 'Maria, what's this?' – This also focuses on one learner and again there is always the risk that she will not know the answer. One way to avoid this is to ask easier questions to weaker learners and harder questions to stronger learners.
4 'What's this?' [teacher waits] 'Yes, Maria.' – This time the teacher waits till someone volunteers an answer. This avoids putting pressure on one learner and gives the whole class a chance to answer. The drawback is that quicker, more confident learners will always answer first.

ACTIVITY 5

– present continuous for talk about actions occurring as we speak – this is an easier concept than the present continuous for arrangements. The form is the same.
– present perfect to talk about a recent event – this is a simpler form (have + past participle) and is used more often, though both have similar uses.

ACTIVITY 7

talk to, talk back, give a talk, talk shop
The most commonly used phrase comes first.

ACTIVITY 8

1 past simple (G)
2 describing people (F)
3 verb phrases with 'go' (V)
4 intonation – rise for questions, fall for decisions. (P)